Flights of Spirit

THE AZRIELI SERIES OF HOLOCAUST SURVIVOR MEMOIRS: PUBLISHED TITLES

ENGLISH TITLES

Flights of Spirit

Elly Gotz

THE AZRIELI FOUNDATION · www.azrielifoundation.org

Cover and book design by Mark Goldstein; Endpaper maps by Martin Gilbert; Map on page xxxix by François Blanc

Document on page 162 courtesy of International Tracing Service (ITS) Bad Arolsen. Photo on page 162 courtesy of United States Holocaust Memorial Museum, courtesy of National Archives and Records Administration, College Park. Photos on page 163 courtesy of Archive Manfred Deiler, European Holocaust Memorial Foundation, Landsberg am Lech. Photos 1 and 2 on page 175 courtesy of Laina Brown and the March of Remembrance and Hope. Cover image of Laisvės Alėja, Kaunas, 1934, courtesy of Kupiškio etnografijos muziejus in Kupiskis, Lithuania.

LIBRARY AND ARCHIVES CANADA CATALOGUING IN PUBLICATION

Gotz, Elly, 1928–, author
    Flights of Spirit/ Elly Gotz.

(Azrieli series of Holocaust survivor memoirs. Series x)
Includes bibliographical references and index.
ISBN 978-1-988065-44-1 (softcover) · 8 7 6 5 4 3 2 1

1. Gotz, Elly, 1928–. 2. Holocaust, Jewish (1939–1945) — Lithuania — Kaunas — Personal narratives. 3. Holocaust survivors — Lithuania — Kaunas — Biography. 4. Holocaust survivors — Canada — Biography. 5. Autobiographies. I. Azrieli Foundation, issuing body II. Title. III. Series: Azrieli series of Holocaust survivor memoirs. Series x

DS135.L53A3 2018   940.53'18092   C2018-905592-8

PRINTED IN CANADA

The Azrieli Series of Holocaust Survivor Memoirs

Naomi Azrieli, Publisher

Jody Spiegel, Program Director
Arielle Berger, Managing Editor
Matt Carrington, Editor
Devora Levin, Assistant Editor
Elizabeth Lasserre, Senior Editor, French-Language Editions
Elin Beaumont, Senior Education Outreach and Program Facilitator
Catherine Person, Bilingual Education and Outreach Coordinator
Stephanie Corazza, Education and Curriculum Associate
Marc-Olivier Cloutier, Bilingual Educational Outreach and Events
　　Assistant
Elizabeth Banks, Digital Asset Curator and Archivist
Susan Roitman, Office Manager (Toronto)
Mary Mellas, Executive Assistant and Human Resources (Montreal)

Mark Goldstein, Art Director
François Blanc, Cartographer
Bruno Paradis, Layout, French-Language Editions

Contents

Series Preface:
In their own words...

In telling these stories, the writers have liberated themselves. For so many years we did not speak about it, even when we became free people living in a free society. Now, when at last we are writing about what happened to us in this dark period of history, knowing that our stories will be read and live on, it is possible for us to feel truly free. These unique historical documents put a face on what was lost, and allow readers to grasp the enormity of what happened to six million Jews — one story at a time.

David J. Azrieli, C.M., C.Q., M.Arch
Holocaust survivor and founder, The Azrieli Foundation

Since the end of World War II, approximately 40,000 Jewish Holocaust survivors have immigrated to Canada. Who they are, where they came from, what they experienced and how they built new lives for themselves and their families are important parts of our Canadian heritage. The Azrieli Foundation's Holocaust Survivor Memoirs Program was established in 2005 to preserve and share the memoirs written by those who survived the twentieth-century Nazi genocide of the Jews of Europe and later made their way to Canada. The program is guided by the conviction that each survivor of the Holocaust has a remarkable story to tell, and that such stories play an important role in education about tolerance and diversity.

Millions of individual stories are lost to us forever. By preserving the stories written by survivors and making them widely available to a broad audience, the Azrieli Foundation's Holocaust Survivor Memoirs Program seeks to sustain the memory of all those who perished at the hands of hatred, abetted by indifference and apathy. The personal accounts of those who survived against all odds are as different as the people who wrote them, but all demonstrate the courage, strength, wit and luck that it took to prevail and survive in such terrible adversity. The memoirs are also moving tributes to people — strangers and friends — who risked their lives to help others, and who, through acts of kindness and decency in the darkest of moments, frequently helped the persecuted maintain faith in humanity and courage to endure. These accounts offer inspiration to all, as does the survivors' desire to share their experiences so that new generations can learn from them.

The Holocaust Survivor Memoirs Program collects, archives and publishes select survivor memoirs and makes the print editions available free of charge to educational institutions and Holocaust-education programs across Canada. They are also available for sale to the general public at bookstores. All revenues to the Azrieli Foundation from the sales of the Azrieli Series of Holocaust Survivor Memoirs go toward the publishing and educational work of the memoirs program.

∼

The Azrieli Foundation would like to express appreciation to the following people for their invaluable efforts in producing this book: Doris Bergen, Manfred Deiler, Christoph Dieckmann, Sherry Dodson (Maracle Inc), Jenn Harris, Rami Neudorfer, and Margie Wolfe & Emma Rodgers of Second Story Press.

About the Glossary

The following memoir contains a number of terms, concepts and historical references that may be unfamiliar to the reader. For information on major organizations; significant historical events and people; geographical locations; religious and cultural terms; and foreign-language words and expressions that will help give context and background to the events described in the text, please see the glossary beginning on page 145.

Introduction

On July 15, 1944, seventeen-year-old Elly Gotz was incarcerated in Kaufering I, a subcamp of the Dachau concentration camp system. Despite the desperate state of the Nazi war effort, the meticulous concentration camp authorities were still recording admission details for each new prisoner that was brought in. Ironically, the Nazis were bringing thousands of Jews from Eastern Europe back to a "Judenrein" Germany as slave labourers, in a doomed attempt to prevent their defeat. Elly is described in an admission document as Eliazar (Eliezer), his traditional Jewish name, as belonging to the Jewish race and to the Jewish religion, and his vocation is listed as *Schlosser*, locksmith. I believe that this description of Elly as a *Schlosser* — a profession that Elly had learned in the vocational school of the Kovno ghetto — symbolizes the way this memoir is a vital key to opening up a piece of history, and can also shape our understanding of Elly's amazing personality and unusual subsequent history.

Elly Gotz was born in the city of Kaunas, Lithuania, on March 8, 1928. Kaunas, known by the Jews as Kovno, was at that time the interim capital of the newly founded Republic of Lithuania. Elly was twelve when the Soviet Union forced independent Lithuania to capitulate and "request" to be annexed to the USSR. He was thirteen when Nazi Germany invaded the Soviet Union and reached his hometown within twenty-four hours. From a relatively worry-free childhood in Lithuania, Elly found himself under Soviet tyranny and then murderous Nazi occupation, was deported back into the Reich, liberated by the Americans and then set out on journeys to Norway, Rhodesia and South Africa — and finally found a home again in Canada.

Elly is a Holocaust survivor: he survived the trials and tribulations of the Kovno ghetto, where he and his family were incarcerated for almost three years; he survived the last ten months of the ghetto's existence, when it was turned over to the SS and run as a brutal concentration camp; and, when Elly and his parents were forcibly deported to concentration camps in Germany, Elly survived the horrible hardships of the Kaufering concentration camp.

According to scholar Dalia Ofer, two things characterized the lives of those incarcerated in ghettos and camps: The inmates lived in a "coerced society," and they were always under the threat of imminent death. Another historian, Lawrence L. Langer, coined the term "choiceless choices" to describe the unprecedented situations of conflict that the Jews found themselves in during the Holocaust. As a result of these conditions, most survivor testimonies read like similar versions of hell: there was the deprivation of much of their humanity, the starvation, the slave labour, the sword of Damocles hanging over their heads, and the understanding that their fate sometimes did not depend on anything they did, which was a debilitating awareness to have.

Yet, as we read Elly's tragic yet fascinating memoir, we get to know a person who played an amazing range of roles in his life. Before the Nazi occupation, during his incarceration in Nazi camps and after liberation, Elly Gotz was, among other things, a mischievous student, a communist Pioneer, an apprentice, a locksmith, a blacksmith, a radio technician, an electric transformer manufacturer, a student of Norwegian, a Zionist activist, a snooker player, a film producer, an animator, an advertiser, a horseback rider and a sharpshooter. He hunted crocodiles, practiced fishing, learned to be a pilot and, recently, at the age of eighty-nine, fulfilled his lifelong wish to become a free-fall skydiver.

But above all, Elly Gotz is dedicated to telling his history. From the first testimony he gave in Munich, on January 4, 1947, to the interviewers of the Central Historical Committee in the occupied American Zone in Germany, until today, Elly has been telling the captivating story of the Shoah and liberation, as he experienced them, to many and varied audiences. He has reached tens of thousands of listeners, mainly students. Elly is a fantastic narrator; his memory is keen, and his knowledge of the events that unfolded between 1940 and 1944 is truly amazing. Seventy-three years after gaining his freedom from Nazi captivity, Elly finally sat down to write his story, one that is deeply embedded in the culture and history of Lithuanian Jews.

Jews in Lithuania: 1915–1940

The terms "Lithuania" and "Lithuanian Jews" can be understood in different ways based on historical, spiritual, cultural and political classifications. Lithuanian Jews, or "Litvaks," as they call themselves, are Jews whose origins are in the territories of present-day Lithuania, Belarus, Latvia, the northeastern parts of Poland and some parts of present-day Russia and Ukraine. Lithuanian Jewry is likewise a religious term — Ashkenazi Jews in Eastern Europe who did not adhere to the Hasidic movement, but rather saw religious studies as the most important aspect of Judaism. Vilnius, Vilna in Yiddish, known in Jewish tradition as *Yerushalayim d'Lita*, Jerusalem of Lithuania, was the traditional centre of Litvak Judaism. There is also a linguistic aspect to the term "Litvak." Lithuanian Jews spoke a distinct dialect of Yiddish, different from the one spoken in other parts of Europe, such as Poland or Ukraine.

Jews began living in Lithuania as early as the tenth century. In 1388 they were granted a charter by Vytautas the Great. After 1792, the Jews became subjects of the czarist Russian Empire, which ruled over Lithuania until 1918. The Russian defeats in World War I and the Russian Revolution caused great suffering to Lithuanian Jews. In 1915, most Lithuanian Jews were forcibly deported to Russia and Ukraine after being falsely accused of collaboration with invading Germans. Shortly after, the Lithuanian territories were conquered by the Germans and remained under German control until February 1918. The Germans tried to placate the Jews by issuing them bilingual passports in German and Yiddish — the first, and probably the only, Yiddish passports in history.

The Russian collapse and the German defeat in 1918 made it possible for the emerging Lithuanian nationalist movement to establish an independent Lithuanian state. On February 16, 1918, the Lithuanians declared independence. In the first provisional government of the Republic of Lithuania, there were three Jewish ministers. A Jewish delegation helped the Lithuanians achieve recognition of their independence in the Congress of Paris, and in return, the Jews received a far-reaching national autonomy, the only one of its kind in Eastern Europe. An interim law allowed the Jews to control all their internal affairs in their national languages: not only religious affairs, but also culture, education, welfare and even the civil registry. Jews were allowed to form their own elected *kehillot*, communities, and to elect their own Nazional-Rat, national council, which reported to a Minister for Jewish Affairs who was Jewish and a member of the Lithuanian cabinet. The communities were allowed to collect their own taxes to finance their activities. Prominent Jews were elected to the Lithuanian parliament, the Seimas.

However, the extensive Jewish national economy did not last long. The right-wing, antisemitic Lithuanian press called the Jewish autonomy "a state within a state," and a new government controlled by right-wing Christian Democrats eroded the powers of the Jewish autonomy. The elected Jewish National Council was disbanded on September 15, 1924.

An attempt to revive the Jewish economy was made in 1926, but on the night of September 17, 1926, right-wing army officers carried out a coup d'état that disbanded the parliament and arrested several democratic leaders. An authoritarian regime headed by Antanas

Smetona came to power and held it until the Soviet annexation in 1940. A series of laws and government initiatives were determined to decrease the economic influence of the Jewish minority. Jews were forbidden from serving in government ministries and the army, and their enrollment in universities was limited. Antisemitism was on the rise, and although the Smetona regime did not follow the Nazi pattern, persecution of the Jews increased.

Kaunas as a Jewish Centre

The city of Kaunas, located at the meeting point of the Nemunas and Viliya rivers, is the second-largest city in Lithuania and the historical centre of Lithuanian economic, political, academic and cultural life. Just before World War I, the city of Kaunas and its suburbs expanded greatly; there were approximately eighty-eight thousand inhabitants in Kaunas, 40 per cent, or approximately forty thousand, of whom were Jews. Most Jews were craftsmen, merchants and owners of small industries. The emerging intelligentsia, such as physicians and lawyers, also included a significant number of Jews.

The Jewish community of independent Lithuania established its own institutions, including welfare organizations such as the Bikur Cholim (Visiting the Sick) hospital. Discriminated against by the government-owned banking system, Jews established their own People's Banks (Folksbenk). The seed money and the banking experience required for the establishment of the Central Jewish Bank in Kovno were provided by the American Jewish Joint Distribution Committee. The Central Bank, where Elly's father, Julius, worked, ran its business in Yiddish, and only 5 per cent of its customers were non-Jews. Jewish traders and manufacturers also formed manufacturing and craft cooperatives, and 75 per cent of businesses were owned by Jews.

There were five Jewish Gymnasiums, or high schools, in Kovno. The first one was the Real Gymnasium, established in 1915 during the German occupation. It was started by Rabbi Dr. Joseph Carlebach, who came to the city as an officer in the German army. The second was the Kaunas Hebrew Gymnasium founded in 1920 (known as "Schwabe," after its famous principal). The Orthodox Yavneh Hebrew Gymnasium for boys was opened in 1928, followed by a separate gymnasium for girls.

Elly Gotz attended the Kommerz Gymnasium, Commerce High School, which belonged to a unique educational movement of Yiddish-speaking schools. These high schools in Lithuania, of which there were only two, were attended mostly by working-class people and by supporters of the Folkist Party, which advocated Jewish autonomy. Supporters of this school system were mostly secular Jews who saw the national language of the Jewish people as Yiddish and not Hebrew. The school was founded in 1926 by the Bildungs-Gesellschaft, an educational society headed by a famous Lithuanian-Jewish leader, Doctor Mendel Sudarsky. Despite its name, the Kommerz Gymnasium had nothing to do with commercial matters. It was a very high-level educational institute with excellent teachers, extensive facilities, laboratories and a wide-ranging and demanding curriculum.

Jewish Kaunas had a thriving cultural and political life. There were dozens of Jewish newspapers and periodicals, many political parties, youth movements, and a people's university for adult education. There were many theatrical productions and two major libraries: the Mapu Library, which had a Zionist Hebrew character, and the Yiddishist Shocharei Daat, Seekers of Knowledge, library. From 1919 to 1940, 109 books in Hebrew were published in Kovno, which included school textbooks, literature, history and books on Judaism.

This golden age in the history of Lithuanian Jewry came to an abrupt end when the Soviets entered the city in June 1940.

Soviet Occupation

The secret arrangement of the Molotov-Ribbentrop Pact, signed just before the outbreak of World War II, divided Eastern Europe into Soviet and Nazi spheres of influence. The eastern part of Poland and the Baltic states belonged to the Soviet zone. The Soviet Union immediately started the process of annexing Lithuania. The first stage was the signing of the Soviet-Lithuanian Mutual Assistance Treaty on October 10, 1939. Lithuania allowed the Soviet state to establish five military bases with twenty thousand troops, and in return received from the Soviets the city of Vilnius and some of the surrounding area. On June 14, 1940, the Soviet government issued an ultimatum to Lithuania demanding it allow an unlimited number of Soviet soldiers to enter the country and form a new pro-Soviet government, later known as the People's Government. President Smetona left the state, and a puppet regime was organized. A puppet parliament was established after sham elections, and the new "People's Seimas" unanimously voted to convert Lithuania into a Soviet Socialist Republic and petition to join the Soviet Union. The Lithuanian request was "graciously approved," and that completed the formalization of the annexation.

The Soviet government started a rapid process of Sovietization, which had a profound effect on Lithuanian life and the economy, on the situation for the Jews and on the relationships between Jews and Lithuanians. In Kovno, 466 businesses, large stores and industrial factories were nationalized, of which 393 belonged to Jews. All houses larger than 220 square metres were also nationalized, and many affluent Jews had to leave their homes. Most Jewish newspapers were shuttered, and in their place the newspapers *Der Emes*, The Truth, and *Shtraln*, Rays, remained. All Zionist parties and youth movements were closed down, as were the Hebrew educational system and cultural institutes.

Most schoolchildren had to go through the trauma of having their school shut down and the language they were taught in completely changed. That was not the case for Elly Gotz. The Commerce High School was allowed to continue and even expand, but its name was changed to Shalom Aleichem, and it moved to the fancier building that had housed the Schwabe Hebrew Gymnasium. The curriculum was changed, however, and Elly had to study the Russian language and the history of the Soviet Union. Since Elly came from a working family and not from the capitalist bourgeoisie, he was allowed to join the Communist Pioneers, a fact of which he was very proud.

On the other hand, Jews also enjoyed great benefits from the new Soviet regime. For the first time in Lithuanian history, they were given equal rights. They were allowed into government positions from which they had been barred, and anti-Jewish discrimination in the universities came to an end. A substantial number of Jews held positions in the Lithuanian Communist Party, and many Jews were members of party organs. This caused immense resentment among the Lithuanian population, and right-wing propaganda accused the Jews of collaborating with the communists and being responsible for the loss of Lithuanian independence. Jews were accused of running the NKVD, the Soviet secret police, which conducted thousands of arrests and deported twelve thousand prominent Lithuanian "suspicious elements" and "enemies of the people" to Siberia. The fact that among these deportees there were many Jews, far beyond their proportion in the country's population, was ignored by the antisemitic groups and their propaganda.

In June 1941 Elly was invited to join the summer camp of the Communist Pioneers in the town of Palanga (called Polangen by the Jews). Elly preferred to stay home with his parents, a fact that likely saved his life. Jewish life in Lithuania was about to be destroyed.

The Outbreak of the War

On Sunday, June 22, 1941, just before dawn, the German invasion of the USSR, Operation Barbarossa, commenced. The German army advanced rapidly from the Baltic to the Black Sea, encountering only light opposition. In most cases, the German invasion enjoyed the full support of the Lithuanian population. Hatred of the Communist regime that had destroyed Lithuanian independence and the belief that Nazi Germany would restore their freedom motivated large groups of Lithuanian nationalists and right-wing extremists to prepare for an armed anti-Soviet rebellion.

Kaunas was taken over by the rebels of the Lithuanian Activist Front (LAF; Lietuvos Aktyvistų Frontas in Lithuanian) who are described by Elly Gotz as "White Armbanders." On June 23, the LAF proclaimed Lithuanian independence and established a provisional government headed by Juozas Ambrazevičius. The provisional government abolished the Soviet government structure and restored capitalism and private property, but not to the Jews. Jews were deprived of their rights and were subject to humiliating and draconian laws; their property was officially confiscated by the Lithuanians.

The Lithuanian nationalists committed horrific atrocities against the city's Jews. On June 25, Lithuanian partisans carried out a horrendous pogrom in the suburb of Slobodka. Eight hundred Jews were murdered, among them many famed rabbis and scholars. One of the most horrific atrocities was committed by Lithuanians in the Lietukis Garage on Vytautas Street. Fifty-two Jews were literally ripped apart by Lithuanians while others watched with delight; no one interfered.

The biggest mass murder carried out by Lithuanian battalions took place at the Seventh Fort outside the city centre. The Lithuanian Provisional Government had set it up as a concentration camp for Jews, and more than ten thousand Jews were taken to the fort in early July. The men were separated from the women and held in horrible conditions outdoors. Many women were beaten, raped and murdered, but on July 14, most of them were released. Only one hundred men who had served in the Lithuanian army during the war for independence in 1919 to 1920 were also set free. The rest, between six and seven thousand, were slain at the Seventh Fort on July 20, 1941.

On August 1, 1941, the Provisional Government of Lithuania started issuing brutal anti-Jewish decrees. Lithuanian Jews were deprived of their citizenship; Jews were forbidden to walk on sidewalks — they were to walk in single file near the gutter; Jews were forbidden to sit on benches in public parks and gardens and were barred from public transport. Every public vehicle had to carry a sign saying "non-Jews only." Jews were prohibited from owning radios or selling their belongings.

Outside the city of Kaunas, the Jews fared an even worse fate. Lithuanian partisans murdered the Jewish inhabitants of 150 towns and villages. As soon as the Germans entered Lithuania, they too began a campaign of annihilation. These murders were aided and abetted by pro-Nazi Lithuanian organizations and Lithuanian auxiliary police. During the summer and autumn of 1941, the Germans killed most of the Jewish population of Lithuania. Only relatively few Jews were allowed to live in three ghettos in the cities of Vilnius, Siauliai and Kaunas.

The Ghetto

From July 2 to August 15, the Jews of Kaunas were ordered to relocate to a ghetto in the suburb of Slobodka (Vilijampolė) across the Viliya River. It was an old, mostly Jewish neighbourhood, which was renowned for its yeshivas. The area of the ghetto had a semi-rural character. Most houses were small wooden shacks with no running water and sometimes without electricity. There were large empty areas between the houses, which had been used by Lithuanian farmers to grow vegetables and fruits. The ghetto area also included significant open spaces near the river. Initially the ghetto was divided into two parts, the large ghetto and the small ghetto, and between them there was a wooden bridge for pedestrians.

On August 4, 1941, an assembly of twenty-eight Jewish public personalities elected a committee to oversee the transfer of the Jews to the ghetto. A noted physician, Dr. Elchanan Elkes, was elected to be the chair of the committee, which subsequently became the Jewish Council of Elders of the Vilijampolė ghetto, the Ältestenrat.

The provisional government of Lithuania was disbanded by the Germans after only six weeks. On August 5, the Germans forced the provisional government to cease its activities and then outlawed the Lithuanian Activist Front. The Nazis formed the entity called Ostland, a huge administrative area that embraced the three Baltic countries and Belorussia. Lithuania was renamed Generalbezirk Litauen,

General District of Lithuania. The district was divided into six *Kreis-gebiete*, districts, one of which was the city of Kaunas, called Kauen-Stadt by the Germans. Kreisgebiet Kauen-Stadt, including the ghetto, was placed under the command of a *Stadt Kommissar*, SA *Brigade-führer* Hans Cramer.

Approximately thirty thousand Jews were forced to move into the ghetto into an area in which formerly only eight thousand people lived, mostly Jews, but also Lithuanians who had to give up their apartments to house the deportees. A frantic search for living space in the ghetto started after the decree was made. Those who had apartments in the city exchanged them with Lithuanians and in return got vastly inferior dwellings. There was not enough space in the new ghetto, and several families had to share one small apartment, one family per room. Poor people and refugees from neighbouring areas who could not find an apartment were housed in *Reservats*, public buildings, under very difficult conditions.

The operation of transferring the Jewish population to the ghetto was facilitated by a Jewish security force that later became the ghetto police (Jüdische Ghetto-Polizei). The members of the Jewish police were usually members of Zionist youth movements, and many of them had served in the army during the Lithuanian Wars of Independence. Contrary to many other police forces in the Jewish ghettos of Eastern Europe, the Jewish police in the Kovno ghetto swore allegiance to the Jewish community and to the Jewish Council. Most of the Jewish police commanders later also became secret leaders of the emerging Jewish underground movements. But despite that, there were cases of favoritism, nepotism and corruption inside the Jewish Council and the police.

The transfer into the Kovno ghetto did not bring any respite to the Jews. On the contrary, there was an endless stream of vicious German decrees designed to humiliate the Jews and rob them of anything they had left. The decrees continued unabated throughout the time they were in the ghetto. One of the first decrees was for Jews to give up their valuables. Under the threat of death, Jews had to hand over gold, silver, jewellery, banknotes, artwork, motor vehicles and animals. They had to give up their bank accounts, promissory notes and stocks and entered the ghetto almost penniless — every Jew was allowed to retain one hundred Soviet rubles or ten German Reichmarks. Nevertheless, many people smuggled gold or precious jewels into the ghetto. However, under the threat of house-to-house searches, most Jews gave up their hidden property and handed it over at collection points in the ghetto. The Germans' take in Slobodka alone exceeded fifty million marks worth of gold and jewellery.

Many more orders followed: In December 1941 Jews had to hand over all their overcoats and furs, which in the harsh winter was a very severe ordinance. In January 1942 Jews had to hand over their pet dogs and cats. These beloved animals were killed by the Germans, their carcasses were thrown into former synagogues and yeshivas and the Jews were forbidden to evacuate the bodies. Jews were also forbidden to pray.

Giving up their property was not the worst difficulty that Jews faced. From the day of the establishment of the ghetto on August 15, 1941, until the end of October 1941, the Germans carried out a series of murderous *Aktionen*, in which about twelve thousand Jews were sent to their deaths, mostly at the Ninth Fort, just outside Kaunas. On the same day the ghetto was established, the Germans lured to their death approximately five hundred Jews from the intelligentsia of the ghetto. They published a false request for people with higher education to do easy administrative work in the city archives. Lawyers, teachers, engineers and other educated people volunteered to go. They were secretly murdered at the Fourth Fort. Several other massacres followed, which Elly describes in his memoir; one murderous scene from the small ghetto stayed with him so strongly that it was the subject of his first eyewitness testimony given after the war.

At the end of October 1941, after three months of relentless murders, only about eighteen thousand Jews remained in the ghetto.

From the pre-war population of about thirty-six thousand, only half remained alive.

After the horrible events of the summer and fall of 1941, in which every single person in the ghetto had lost family members or friends, the situation calmed down somewhat for a period of about two years. This time is known as the calm or stable period, because between October 1941 and October 1943 there were no large-scale killings, and the state of affairs in the ghetto was relatively static.

The Nature of the Ghetto

A few days after the establishment of the ghetto, in the second half of August 1941, the Council of Elders issued the founding statutes of the ghetto community. I have discovered that these statutes were based on the regulations of the previously mentioned 1920 Jewish national autonomy. This important document established the principles for the operations of the Jewish Council, which would see to all aspects of life in the ghetto — public order, provision of lodging, food, health, social security, religious and cultural needs, legal services and the establishment of economic enterprises. A very unusual document, it read like a declaration of full autonomy and authority over the whole Jewish population. What is strange in this document is what is missing: the statutes totally ignore the state of war, the liquidation of half the population and the slave labour that all adult inmates of the ghetto were obliged to perform six days a week.

There is an inherent conflict between the way the Nazi rulers saw the council and how they saw themselves. The council saw itself as the leadership of a *kehillah*, a traditional Jewish community. The Nazis saw the council as a body that would carry out their orders and provide slave labour for the Nazi war effort.

It is important to understand why the Nazis liquidated almost all Lithuanian Jews and why they then relented and kept some of them alive, caged in three ghettos. In warring with the Soviet Union, the Germans had planned a quick *Blitzkrieg*, in which the Soviet Union would be brought to its knees and surrender within a few weeks. Soon, though, the Germans realized that their plans for a swift victory would not materialize. The Soviet Union was crushed, but it did not capitulate. The endless Soviet reserves and their strategic depth promised a long war, for which the German war machine was not prepared. They desperately needed labourers to support their efforts. Initially, they used the hundreds of thousands of Soviet prisoners of war, but they treated these prisoners so badly, not giving them shelter or food, that most of them died. And so, the remaining Jews in Lithuania were seen as essential workers for the Nazi war effort.

Slave Labour

At first, most Jews had to perform harsh slave labour at the Aleksotas Aerodrome, the new military airport the German air force was trying to build closer to the front. This work was exacting and dangerous — workers were beaten, and some were even killed by supervisors. Thousands of Jews worked in the Aerodrome.

Gradually, the Germans were convinced that it would be more effective to use skilled Jewish workers. More workplaces were created: workshops and factories, peat mines, logging sites, military camps and office work in the headquarters of the SS Security Police. Groups called "the city brigades" were marched in columns daily to the workplace and back. Some of these sites were remote and harsh, but others made for easier work that was done indoors. What was most significant about the workplaces in the city was that they provided the opportunity for illegal black-market trade with Lithuanians. Under the threat of death, the workers took with them their remaining fine clothes or some valuables they had managed to keep and traded them for precious food. They smuggled this food back into the ghetto to feed the members of their households, which was very dangerous. From time to time they were caught by the ghetto guards, although it was sometimes possible to bribe the guards. If food was found hidden

by the incoming workers, they were beaten, thrown in jail or sometimes turned over to the Gestapo. In some cases, the impounded food
was given back to the Jewish Council who then distributed it to the
social aid kitchen or to the special kitchen for the aerodrome workers
who could not trade with the locals.

Soon, a new type of workplace was added. At the initiative of the
economic department of the Jewish Council, the "big workshops"
were set up. These workshops were supposed to utilize the skills of
Jewish tailors, shoemakers, carpenters, tinsmiths, locksmiths, toy-
makers and other craftspeople. Officially, the articles produced in
these workshops were meant for use in the German war effort. In
reality, private German and Lithuanian enterprises often bribed their
way into employing these artisans for their personal gain or for the
manufacture of gifts that they sent to chosen recipients — such as
toys to their children or gifts to family in Germany.

The Book Action

Most ghetto survivors remember as especially distressing the decree
that was issued on February 26, 1942, known as the Book Action.
On that date, the Council of Elders published a decree in Lithuanian
and Yiddish that stated that the occupation authorities had ordered
ghetto inhabitants to hand over all books in their possession; houses
would be searched, and if people were found with books they would
be severely punished.

The confiscation of Jewish cultural treasures and books had started in the German Reich after the infamous night of Kristallnacht in
November 1938. After the start of the war, the mission to confiscate
Jewish treasures was assigned to specific task forces; the books collected by officials all over Eastern Europe were supposed to become
the basis for a research library and museum that would record the
culture of the non-existent Jewish race. The Book Action was also
intended, of course, to deliver a spiritual blow to the Jewish popula-

tion, to rob them of their cultural heritage and deprive them of any opportunity for cultural activities or education.

Most ghetto inhabitants complied with the book order. Some groups, such as the Orthodox and communist organizations, tried to defy the order by keeping a small number of culturally important books and maintaining hidden libraries. Elly Gotz and his father committed a very dangerous act of resistance by rescuing many books that other Jews had handed over and building a secret library that provided young Elly with an education and a connection to culture.

Education

One of the most fascinating parts of Elly's memoirs is his detailed description of the time he spent at the vocational school in the ghetto, which played a major role in his life and his survival. The initiative to found a vocational school in the ghetto started at the beginning of 1942. Hundreds of youngsters were doing harsh physical labour at the aerodrome and other places. Others strolled idly about the ghetto or worked as "angels" (illegal substitutes for adult workers). It was thought that a vocational school would teach the young people skills that would help them get work under more favorable conditions in the ghetto workshops. The school was staffed by the pre-war teachers and instructors of ORT (the Organization for Rehabilitation through Training) School in Kaunas. The head of the vocational school was Dr. Jacob Oleiski, the previous principal of the ORT school network in independent Lithuania and under Soviet dominion. Two main problems stood in the way of the establishment of the school: The first was finding a suitable location in the over-populated space, and the second was finding tools and materials for the classes. One of the cement blocks of the ghetto, Block C, was renovated and converted into a space that could serve as the vocational school. Elly describes the first days of the school and how the pupils dug through the rubble of the ghetto and in the remains of former schools and workshops to uncover tools for the new school.

The first class at the vocational school, the locksmithing class, was opened in March 1942 with thirty pupils, Elly among them. The second class, carpentry, opened in April. Other classes, such as metal work and bricklaying, followed, as well as sewing for the girls. By summer 1942, there were 150 pupils at the school. A specialized learning program was organized for all children between the ages of ten and thirteen. The older children worked for four to five hours and then had about two to three hours of theoretical studies in fields like mathematics, technology and mechanics.

Elly's description of his time spent at the school is both moving and entertaining. As a historian, I found his description of the establishment of the school and the methods of teaching extremely important for my research. Elly was an outstanding student and instructor and has very warm memories of the two years he spent there, and rightly so. School pupils were protected from the horrors of the outside world and the everyday mortal dangers facing the ghetto inhabitants. Many special events and cultural activities were organized at the school. There was a children's choir, a mandolin orchestra, special concerts and cultural events.

Even when the ghetto was officially shut down in October 1943 and turned over to the SS and declared a concentration camp, the vocational school activities continued as before. In February 1944, the school reached its maximum number of 440 students. Among those were children between eight and ten years old who were given false ID cards stating their age as twelve, the minimum age for compulsory slave labour. These falsified identity cards did not help all the children during the horrific Children's Action in March 1944. On March 27 and 28, approximately one thousand children — fifty-four of whom were the younger schoolchildren — were murdered by the

Nazis, along with the elderly and sick, at the Ninth Fort or were deported to Auschwitz.[1]

Cultural Activities

Music was the most significant cultural activity in the ghetto. A group of very talented musicians were given fictitious jobs in the Jewish police in order to protect them from harsh physical labour. In 1942 the musicians decided to form a ghetto orchestra, which was directed by Michael Hofmekler, a renowned conductor and musician before the war. Between November 1942 and October 1943, about ninety concerts were held, which were greatly enjoyed by most of the ghetto population. Despite that, there was some opposition to holding festive concerts in the ghetto. Religious groups, as well as the communist underground, thought it was inappropriate to hold concerts after so many of the ghetto inhabitants had been murdered.

One of the most important cultural events in the history of the ghetto took place on July 24, 1943. It was a secret Zionist concert in which members of the ghetto leadership and the Zionist groups gathered together and sang Hebrew songs. At the end of this very moving event, the audience sang together the Zionist anthem "Hatikva" (The Hope), which was to become the national anthem of the State of Israel five years later. The programs and the musical scores of many of those concerts were buried underground with the rest of the ghetto archives, some of which were recovered after the war.

---

1 On that day all the members of the Jewish ghetto police were taken to the Ninth Fort and tortured. The Germans wanted to get information about where children were hiding and the whereabouts of the ghetto archives, which were hidden by the police officers who handled them. About 38 of the 140 police members were tortured to death, but did not reveal the information. Other policemen, though, broke under torture and revealed some hiding places. The Jewish ghetto police was disbanded. In its place, a smaller police force, the Ordnungsdienst, was established. While the first police force was loyal to the community and to the Council of Elders, the new one was composed of collaborators and criminals who helped the SS in their efforts to hunt down Jews in hiding.

Germans would take them for forced labour. The Gotz family, who were in hiding, eventually decided to emerge and boarded the trains to the concentration camps in Germany. The Jews who did not believe the Germans and stayed in their hiding places were mostly murdered, their hiding places set on fire or blown up. Only about 150 Jews managed to hide in the ghetto until their liberation on August 1, 1944.

Two shipments of Jews were taken out of the former Kovno ghetto on July 12, 1944. They were loaded onto cattle cars that carried them all the way to a small railway station called Tiegenhof, in eastern Prussia, where they were separated by gender. The women and girls were taken off the train and transported to the Stutthof concentration camp, while the men and boys continued on to Bavaria, in Germany, ultimately reaching the vast concentration camp complex of Dachau.

After 1943, the Dachau camp system had grown to include nearly a hundred subcamps, which were mostly work camps (*Arbeitskommandos*) and were located throughout southern Germany and Austria. Most prisoners from the Kovno ghetto were incarcerated in the Kaufering subcamp system, which included eleven camps located near the city of Landsberg. Life in the concentration camp was very harsh — the work, treatment, food supply and living conditions were far worse than in the KZ Kauen. The prisoners slept on hard wooden boards inside flimsy, temporary structures; food rations were much below the minimum required for subsistence; the clothing handed out by the SS was totally inadequate, especially in winter; and working conditions were brutal, also especially in winter, with people dying from exposure and from falling into the wet concrete.

The prisoners were involved in a doomed project: an immense effort to miraculously save the crumbling Nazi state. Codenamed "Weingut II," the plan was to build a huge underground factory for production of Germany's newest aircraft — the jet-powered Messerschmitt Me 262. The Messerschmitt was the world's first jet fighter and far superior to any Allied piston-engined fighter aircraft then in service. However, the Germans could not produce this aircraft in sufficient quantities because of the Allies' total air superiority over Western Europe, so they planned to cast massive half-buried reinforced concrete bunkers. The ambitious German plan was to use ninety thousand slave labourers in three plants all over Germany to assemble nine hundred jet fighters a month. There were three or four such bunkers in Germany, and the one Elly describes was the nearest to completion. However, by the end of the war, in April 1945, even this concrete bunker was not complete, and not a single jet aircraft was made in that enormous effort.

Return to Life

In the first few weeks after liberation, Elly's thoughts were directed toward exacting revenge against the Germans. He was not alone in having these thoughts. Several groups of Holocaust survivors and Jewish soldiers planned and sometimes executed revenge. Elly, though, came to his senses and realized that hate would hold him back from concentrating on his future.

Only after liberation were people able to slowly recover and rediscover their humanity. They started to face significant dilemmas and issues: finding a place to live and a career; trying to fill in gaps in their education; finding their families or starting new ones; and, most importantly, finding meaning in life after their horrible losses. In that sense, the lucky few who made it to liberation are all different. Some were broken by their personal tragedies and never recovered, while others were emboldened by their struggles. Elly's story is a tale of salvation and success.

Unlike his war story, Elly's post-war story is no longer a history in the common sense of the word. It is his own private story full of wonders and achievements. Elly completed his studies, worked in many interesting and sometimes weird and entertaining jobs, found his future wife, raised children and grandchildren and found his permanent home in Canada. In Canada, Elly has been a successful entrepreneur and social activist.

Throughout his life, Elly has neither forgotten his roots nor the horrible time that he went through between 1941 and 1945, and he continues to give hundreds of lectures to many thousands of listeners. This important book that you will be reading is a memorial to the blessed souls of the victims of Nazi brutality, and in a way that is emblematic of Elly's initial profession, unlocks a part of Elly's history, of who he is and why.

Rami Neudorfer is writing a dissertation about the inner life of the Kovno ghetto.
2018

SOURCES AND SUGGESTED READING

Abramovich, Solomon and Yaakov Zilberg. *Smuggled in Potato Sacks: Fifty Stories of the Hidden Children of the Kaunas Ghetto.* London; Portland, OR: Vallentine Mitchell, 2011.

Aly, Götz, et al. "Das Baltikum unter deutscher Zivilverwaltung." *Die Verfolgung und Ermordung der europäischen Juden durch das nationalsozialistische Deutschland 1933–1945* 7, no. 7. Oldenbourg, 2011.

Arad, Yitzhak. "The Judenräte in the Lithuanian Ghettos of Kovno and Vilna." *Patterns of Jewish Leadership in Nazi Europe,1933–1945: Proceedings of the Third Yad Vashem International Historical Conference, April 4-7, 1977.* Jerusalem: Yad Vashem (1979): 93–112.

Benz, Wolfgang, K. Kwiet, and J. Matthäus. *Einsatz im "Reichskommissariat Ostland": Dokumente zum Völkermord im Baltikum und in Weißrussland 1941–1944.* Berlin, 1998.

Bubnys, Arūnas. *Kaunas Ghetto 1941–1944.* Vilnius: Genocide and Resistance Research Centre of Lithuania, 2014.

Cohen, Sharon Kangisser. "The Experience of the Jewish Family in the Nazi Ghetto: Kovno — A Case Study." *Journal of Family History* 31, no. 3 (2006): 267-288.

Dieckmann, Christoph. *Deutsche Besatzungspolitik in Litauen 1941-1944.* 2 vols. Goettingen: Wallstein, 2011.

Eilati, Shalom. *Crossing the River.* Tuscaloosa: University of Alabama Press, 2008.

Elkes, Joel. *Values, Belief and Survival: Dr. Elkhanan Elkes and the Kovno Ghetto*. London: Vale, 1997.

Frasier, Slaten, and Amanda Marie. "Schooling in the Kovno Ghetto: Cultural Reproduction as a Form of Defiance." *Paedagogica Historica: International Journal of the History of Education* 51 (2015): 197–205.

Ganor, Solly. *Light One Candle: A Survivor's Tale from Lithuania to Jerusalem*. New York: Kodansha International, 1995.

Ginaite-Rubinson, Sara. *Resistance and Survival: The Jewish Community in Kaunas 1941–1944*. Oakville, Ontario: Mosaic Press, 2005. Kindle edition.

Hilberg, Raul. "The Ghetto as a Form of Government." *Annals of the American Academy of Political and Social Science* 450 (July 1980): 98–112.

Kaubrys, Saulius. "Was the Jewish community of Kaunas exceptional?" *Transversal* 11, no. 1 (2010): 87–102.

Levin, Dov. "How the Jewish Police in the Kovno Ghetto Saw Itself." *Yad Vashem Studies* (2001): 183–240.

Liekis, Šarūnas. *A State within a State? Jewish Autonomy in Lithuania, 1918–1925*. Vilnius: Versus aureus, 2003.

Littman, Sol. *War Criminal on Trial: The Rauca Case*. Toronto: Lester and Orpan, 1983.

Michman, Dan. *The Emergence of Jewish Ghettos during the Holocaust*. Cambridge, MA: Cambridge University Press, 2011.

Mishell, William W. *Kaddish for Kovno: Life and Death in a Lithuanian Ghetto, 1941–1945*. Chicago: Chicago Review Press, 1988.

Ofer, Dalia. "Ghetto Inmates: Their Perspectives and the Historian's Craft." *Lebenswelt Ghetto* (2013): 52–70.

Porat, Dina. "The Holocaust in Lithuania: Some Unique Aspects." In *The Final Solution: Origins and Implementation*, 159–175. London: Routledge, 1994.

Porat, Dina. "Zionists and Communists in the Underground during the Holocaust: Three Examples — Cracow, Kovno and Minsk." *Journal of Israeli History* 18, no. 1 (1997): 57–72.

Schalkowsky, Samuel, trans. and ed. *The Clandestine History of the Kovno Jewish Ghetto Police: By Anonymous Members of the Kovno Jewish Ghetto Police*. Bloomington: Indiana University Press and the United States Holocaust Memorial Museum, 2014.

Shavit, David. *Hunger for the Printed Word: Books and Libraries in the Jewish Ghettos of Nazi-Occupied Europe*. Jefferson: McFarland, 1997.

Tauber, Joachim. *Arbeit als Hoffnung: Jüdische Ghettos in Litauen 1941–1944*. Berlin: De Gruyter, 2015.

Tory, Avraham, Martin Gilbert, and Dina Porat. *Surviving the Holocaust: The Kovno Ghetto Diary*. Cambridge, MA: Harvard University Press, 1990.

Trunk, Isaiah. "The Jewish Councils in Eastern Europe under Nazi Rule (An Attempt at a Synthesis)." *Societas* 2, no. 3 (1972): 221–239.

United States Holocaust Memorial Museum. *Hidden History of the Kovno Ghetto*. Edited by Dennis B. Klein. Boston: Little, Brown and Co., 1997.

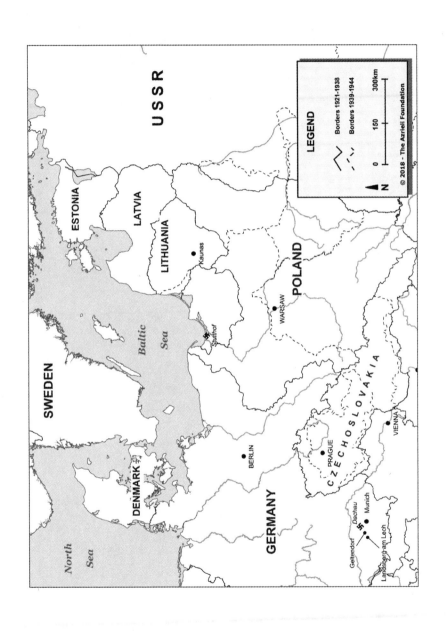

LEGEND

Borders 1921-1938

Borders 1939-1944

0   150   300km

N

USSR

SWEDEN

ESTONIA

LATVIA

LITHUANIA

Kaunas

Baltic Sea

Stutthof

WARSAW

POLAND

North Sea

DENMARK

BERLIN

GERMANY

CZECHOSLOVAKIA

PRAGUE

VIENNA

Geltendorf

Dachau

Munich

Landsberg am Lech

Acknowledgements

I recall with love the people who, during the terrible years of 1941–1945, made my survival possible: My dear parents, Judel and Sonja Gotz, my uncles Gedalie, David and his wife, Mary, and Tanchum Wilentschuk.

The training I received from ORT in the ghetto contributed substantially to my survival in Dachau, and, after liberation, my training through ORT in radio mechanics helped me transition to normal life.

I am grateful to the family members who took my parents and me out of Europe to a new life in Southern Africa. My father's brother Samuel Gotz and his wife, Ann, in Southern Rhodesia (now Zimbabwe), and my father's Uncle Isaac Liknaitzky of Johannesburg, South Africa, who enabled me to fulfill my dream and attend university in Johannesburg.

Writing this book turned out to be a greater challenge than I anticipated. When I showed my wife, Esme, my initial attempts at telling my story, her comment was: "You write like an engineer! Where are the *feelings*?" Well, I am an engineer, but I did not know there is an engineering style of writing! She began to interview me and wrote several pages while constantly asking, "How did you feel at that moment?" I struggled with "feelings" and I tried my best to improve my style. Thank you, dear Esme, for your help and encouragement.

This being my first experience of writing a book, I was surprised and amazed at the essential contribution of my editor, Arielle Berger, the Managing Editor of the memoirs program. She wove the touching letters my parents wrote from Europe into the text with great skill. She shaped the structure of the content to make it a book. I express my gratitude to her skill and patience. I also thank Christopher Warren, who helped me in the initial stages by improving my writing style.

Rami Neudorfer of Israel checked many of the historical details of my text and suggested corrections. He also wrote the introduction, giving the historical framework within which my life experiences played out. Thank you, Rami Neudorfer!

I want to also thank the teachers who, over many years, invited me to inspire their students with a deeper understanding of the Holocaust. While doing so, I have become close friends with many teachers and continue to marvel at their dedication to their craft.

Thanks are due as well to Jody Spiegel, the director of the whole Holocaust Survivor Memoirs Program, and to Elin Beaumont, the Senior Educational Outreach & Events Coordinator.

I wish to express my deep gratitude and appreciation to the Azrieli Foundation for publishing my book in English and, later, in French. My book will join a large library of Holocaust survivor memoirs created so generously by the Azrieli Foundation. It will be the raw material for future generations of writers and poets who will ensure that this human tragedy will live in the memory of humankind.

Above all, my life has been inspired by my dear wife, Esme, my children, Ruven and Deborah, Julia and Nathan, and Avril and Martin, and my beloved grandchildren, Anita, Ilana, Ethan, Sarah, Martin and Robin.

People should write their biographies, particularly in times when truth was stranger than fiction.

Stefan Zweig

Syringes on a Tray

The most dramatic event in my life happened in the summer of 1944. I was sixteen years old, and I was facing my death. In wartime, death can occur at any time. But on this day, death would come not from the hand of my enemy — it would come from the hand of my beloved mother.

I was hiding in a basement with my mother, my father, my three uncles and my aunt. We had covered the entrance to the room with an old cupboard, and we sat there listening to every sound coming from outside. We had all agreed that we would rather die here than be captured and shot on the killing fields of the Ninth Fort in Kaunas, Lithuania.

My mother, who was a surgical nurse in the ghetto hospital, had been given the task of arranging our communal suicide. She had filled several syringes with a potent heart drug. The plan was to inject an excessive dose of the drug in our veins and cause a heart attack.

I watched my mother as she prepared a serving tray covered with a clean white cloth. On the tray, there was a bottle of medical alcohol, and beside each syringe lay a ball of cotton wool. I thought this was funny, so I reminded my mother that as this was a final injection, it did not have to be a clean one. Everyone laughed except my mother, but she took away the cotton wool.

It was very boring to sit for days on end in that dim basement. I had a lot of time to think and I had many questions: How does it feel to die? Does the brain go on working for a time after the heart stops? My mother was a strong woman and I trusted her, but would she have the strength to give me, her only child, the first injection?

I tried to imagine my mother injecting the six of us and then, finally, herself. Then I tried to imagine the seven of us lying on the floor waiting for the drug to kick in. What would we say to each other? Would we laugh or cry? Would it be painful? As I tried to picture the scene, I decided it would be good to go first — I did not wish to see it.

I will now try to describe the circumstances that would make a woman like my mother ready to kill her son and her family. This story can only be understood after knowing what was happening in the Kaunas ghetto during the three years we were imprisoned there.

Mischievous Childhood

First, I want to tell you a little about Lithuania. It is a small country on the Baltic Sea, close to Latvia and Estonia. The capital city during my childhood was Kaunas, which was known by the Jews as Kovno. That is the city where I was born and where I grew up. Some people called it Little Paris. During the fall and winter there were performances by Kovno's own ballet, theatre and opera companies.

For me, life was beautiful. I was an only child, and though I wouldn't say I was spoiled, I was certainly indulged. I had a bicycle, I had friends and I went to a private school. In the summer I went to the seaside or spent time at a cottage on a farm.

My father, Julius (Judel), was born in Šiauliai (Shavel), Lithuania, in 1891. He dreamt of becoming an engineer and pursued his dreams by studying engineering at the Petrograd Peter the Great Polytechnic Institute in Saint Petersburg, Russia. It had been extremely difficult to get into the famous university — Jews were not desired there, and historically, had not even been allowed to live in Saint Petersburg. It took amazing drive to get in, and there was much suffering along the way. My father was greatly inspired by his socialist revolutionary older cousins, Mikhail and Abraham Gotz, whom he used to visit in Moscow. Unfortunately, his cousins were arrested for trying to bring down the Czarist regime, and they were sent to Siberia for many years. My father, meanwhile, was caught up in a crucial epoch of Russian history — the Russian Revolution, a time when chaos and total anarchy erupted and universities were closed down. My father was in his second year of electrical engineering when he had to flee, and he was never able to return to his studies and become an engineer. Instead, he came back to Lithuania and found work as a bookkeeper in the Central Jewish Bank (Centralinis žydų bankas), a cooperative in Kaunas that gave small loans to Jews, unlike the other banks in Lithuania.

My father loved math, science and technology. I was lucky that he shared his enthusiasms with me. Every week, he would take me to the library to borrow books. We also carefully selected books to buy. I was proud of my personal collection of historical novels, biographies of famous people, travel books and books on science.

My mother, on the other hand, loved literature, theatre and the arts. Again, I was fortunate that she shared her interests with me. She loved music and opera and had a good voice herself. She introduced me to opera, classical music and wonderful storybooks. My mother was a very attractive woman and had a presence that always evoked respect. She had a point of view on many issues that was based on a worldly and liberal outlook derived from literature and art. She was fluent in Yiddish, Russian, Lithuanian and German, read a great deal and was familiar with the greats of world literature.

Born in Kaunas in 1902, my mother, Sonja, experienced her first refugee status in 1915, when all Kaunas Jews were exiled from the city and moved deep into Russia. The Czar regarded them as possible allies of Germany in World War 1 and wanted the Jews away from the border with Germany. Returning to Lithuania in 1918, my mother finished high school and was trained as a pediatric nurse. She worked in the Kovno Jewish hospital, Bikur Cholim, and later in an orphanage established by the Jewish community for war orphans. There she met my father, Julius, who worked as a volunteer in the orphanage, and they married in 1926.

When I was born, on March 8, 1928, I was named Eliezer, but everyone called me Elly. My mother decided to give up nursing and work from home. She took a course in dressmaking at the ORT (Organization for Rehabilitation through Training), a Jewish vocational school in Kaunas, and opened a dressmaking workshop in our apartment, designing and sewing dresses to augment the family income.

We were not wealthy, and my parents worried about their incomes, but I was not aware of this as a child. I was not lacking anything. I was the only grandchild of two sets of loving grandparents, Joshua and Bluma Gotz, and my maternal grandparents, Shlomo and Alte Wilentschuk. My maternal grandmother's name was Chaya Leah (née Schwartz), but I called her by her nickname, Alte (old one), given to her when she was young and very sick in the hopes that the new name would help her heal. I was also the only nephew of four uncles, three on my mother's side living in Kaunas — Tanchum, David and Gedalie Wilentschuk, who was managing director of the orphanage where my mother worked— and my father's brother, Samuel Gotz, who was living in Southern Rhodesia (now called Zimbabwe), Africa.

I was familiar with several languages while I was growing up. My parents spoke Yiddish to me at home, and when they didn't want me to understand what they were saying, they spoke Russian. It didn't take me long to learn Russian from those conversations that were supposed to go over my head! When I went downstairs to play in the yard with other kids, I spoke Lithuanian, which was taught at school along with German. I also had lots of opportunity to practice my German with the many neighbours and friends who spoke it. As if four languages were not enough, I also had to learn Hebrew, since Jews pray in Hebrew.

I attended a private school for Jewish children called Kommerz Gymnasia, where everything was taught in Yiddish. The Yiddish language is about a thousand years old and is rich in literature and poetry. My parents were proponents of Yiddish culture and were politically inclined to the liberal left, a stance that my school supported. I was a good student and usually had top marks or very high marks. I loved mathematics and reading about history and science. My main hobby was building model airplanes, which helped me develop fine motor skills. I dreamed of one day becoming an engineer and a pilot.

When walking home from school, I learned to be cautious. Some of the Lithuanian gentile youths were antisemitic, and I knew that some of these rougher kids might attack me for being a Jew, particularly if I was alone. I wasn't a fighter, so to avoid them I would choose a route that I felt was safe. I accepted these problems as part of my life.

On my way to school there was a temptation — a soda stand. I loved soda water with cherry juice, but the pocket money I received from my parents would cover only two drinks a week. So, every day I had to decide whether I really wanted the soda right then, or whether the desire would be even more urgent the next day. I believe that this daily internal debate taught me to save money. I once read a definition of an entrepreneur as a person who delays present pleasure (spending) for future pleasure, again and again.

At school I loved doing science and chemistry experiments, and I wanted to try doing experiments on my own as well. I had test tubes and a little burner, and I managed to repeat an experiment I was shown in school: boil a green leaf in alcohol in a test tube, then let it cool and settle. The green chlorophyll gathers clearly on top of the tube. At the bottom, the brown colour of a leaf in autumn appears, showing that the brown colour is already present in the leaf when the green disappears. I thought that was neat to observe!

When I was about ten years old, I had an idea to make a stink match. When the match was lit, it would produce an acrid smoke, confounding those present. I collected some lab equipment and began my research. Using regular wood matches, I coated their heads with my proprietary mixture of materials and then dried them in the oven at a low heat. My mixture consisted of artists' white oil paint mixed with ink, and chalk shavings to give it consistency. Sometimes I added my mother's face cream to the mixture. When I lit one or two matches, the smoke in the room was quite unpleasant. I began to sell the matches to my school friends, who all managed to upset their elders by lighting the matches, then walking out of the room and letting others discover the smell.

To test my products I used our toilet room, which had no windows. Usually I did my testing in the afternoons, when there was no one in the apartment. But one day a relative walked in just after one of my tests, and the small room was full of acrid smoke. She jumped up, shouting, "Fire!" My mother came running, and I assured her that there was no fire and that the smoke was just from my experiment. But when my father got home, my mother told him to find my laboratory box, which was under my bed, and get rid of it. Father wanted to throw the wooden box with my materials into a fire, but my mother loudly objected, saying that it might explode! That was the end of my first profitable business.

Another activity was going out with my friend Shaya, who had similar interests to mine, to look for interesting wildlife in the rivers around the city. We fitted ourselves out with bottles attached to our belts with string and little nets. We caught frogs, water bugs and leeches. I knew better than to bring them home, so we went to Shaya's house and observed them there. One day the leeches escaped! His mother found one on her body and nearly had a heart attack. That night, she was too scared to sleep. So, we stopped our "science," but we found another occupation after school — going to the railway shunting yard. There, a small locomotive went to and fro, moving the freight wagons from one place to another for loading or unloading. First, we learned to jump on and off a slow-moving rail car. To do it safely you needed to jump off while facing forward yet, at the same time, push yourself backward to reduce the speed of landing on the ground. We practiced it many times until we could jump off safely at higher speeds.

Then we discovered that most freight wagons came with a lead seal attached to a thin rope on the doors. The rope had to be cut when unloading the cargo. Many seals remained hanging on the doors after the string was cut on one side. We began to collect the lead seals;

then we made a fire and melted the lead and cast it into sand or clay moulds. We made fishing sinker weights and other little figurines. If the sand mould had water in it, the hot lead would cause the water to explode into bursts of steam, shooting bits of lead upward. I understand now how dangerous that was.

If our parents had known what we were up to, they would have had a fit!

The Path of Destruction

Prior to the onset of World War II in September 1939, Germany and the Soviet Union secretly became allies. They made an agreement, later called the Molotov-Ribbentrop Pact, to divide Eastern Europe into German and Soviet spheres of influence. Lithuania, along with Latvia, Estonia and parts of Romania and Finland, fell into the Soviet sphere; Poland was divided between Germany and the Soviet Union. In the summer of 1940, the Soviet Union forced Lithuania into its orbit by demanding that Lithuania become a Soviet republic. Thousands of Soviet soldiers were stationed throughout the country.

The Soviet occupation caused a tremendous upheaval in Lithuania. Employees of all companies were required to attend communist political training meetings. Businesses were either closed — as was the bank my father worked at — or taken over by the Soviets. My father had to find a new job. People who owned property or who were considered wealthy — the bourgeois or elite — could be banished to Siberia. Anyone who resisted or spoke against the new Communist regime was treated harshly.

Changes were made to our school curriculum. Now our school was called Shalom Aleichem, and we were taught the Russian language. We had to study the history of the Soviet Union and the Communist Party. At the time, I was proud to be accepted into the Young Pioneers group, which was like the Boy Scout movement, but with a communist indoctrination. I was also happy to wear the red tie they gave me. I was in Grade 6 and my life essentially continued as before.

But in the summer of 1941, my life changed completely. Every summer, I looked forward to a vacation outside the city. Our family would rent a summer house somewhere beautiful, inland or by the sea. By the summer of 1941, under the new regime, this was no longer financially possible.

The Young Pioneers had organized a summer camp in the town of Palanga, by the Baltic Sea. As a member of the Pioneers I was eligible to attend, and my parents suggested that I take the opportunity to get out of the city. But I did not want to go, and my parents accepted my decision. Although antisemitism was officially forbidden under the Soviet regime, I knew that the local gentile kids would use every opportunity to gang up on the Jewish kids. I suspected that the teaching of equality had not yet sunk in deeply enough with some people. I had a bad feeling about that camp, but I could not have foreseen what kind of a disaster it would turn out to be.

On June 22, 1941, the German army, without even declaring war, crossed the border into the Soviet Union, ending their pact of nearly two years. I heard that German soldiers reached the Pioneer camp that same day and that right away, the soldiers asked whether there were Jews in the camp. Apparently, some gentile kids were immediately willing to point out their Jewish comrades. Most of the Jewish children were taken away and eventually shot and murdered, and I lost several of my school friends. One of them was Eli Goldstein.

My friend in Toronto, Abby Beker, a Holocaust survivor like me, was in that camp as well. When he saw that the Jews were being singled out, he jumped over a fence and took off by foot. It took him a week to make the trek back to Kaunas through side roads and by getting rides on horse-driven wagons.

I was thirteen years old and my life, so regular and tranquil until then, had suddenly turned; I could not have anticipated how drastically. I had been looking forward to starting high school that

September, and my parents had ordered my new school uniform — a black suit with a stiff collar. I felt very proud in that uniform, and I had an official photograph taken, a copy of which was sent to my uncle in Africa. Thanks to him, I have a record of that moment in my life. Sadly, I never got to wear my school uniform; my school never reopened, and I never got to attend high school.

~

When the German army entered Lithuania in June 1941, they encountered little or no resistance. The local population was pleased to see the backs of the communist Soviets and were almost welcoming to the German army. As soon as the Soviets left, the Lithuanians hurriedly established a provisional government in the hope that Germany would permit Lithuania to become independent again, as it had been in 1939. This was not to be.

Among the first laws passed by the Lithuanian Provisional Government was the law that Jews were not Lithuanian citizens and had no rights whatsoever. That is when the attacks on the Jews began. Vicious individuals and groups of so-called "partisans" delighted in robbing and killing Jews. Local Lithuanian nationalist gangs, whom we called White Armbanders, brutally murdered hundreds of Jews during the first days of the occupation. Between June 25 and 27, 1941, a savage massacre of helpless people, a pogrom, took place in Kaunas, followed by a second pogrom two days later.

I felt the fear in my parents, a fear that was relentless, day and night. They worried constantly that they would be dragged out of the house and killed, which was happening to people we knew.

Soon after the pogroms, between June 30 and July 7, the White Armbanders yanked approximately five thousand Jews from their homes and locked them up in the Seventh Fort, a military compound surrounded by brick walls. Over several days, all the men were murdered. Some women were shot, while others were released.

The Lithuanian Provisional Government lasted for six weeks until the German authorities shut it down and established control over the country. Lithuania was now on another path of destruction. When Jews were ordered to walk in the gutters, my mother's proud bearing prompted a Nazi officer to bark at her, "Don't walk so proud, Jewess!"

That summer, the Germans announced that all Jews must move from their homes in the community and relocate to a designated area. The Germans claimed that this was to protect the Jews from attacks by the local population; in fact, this gave them the opportunity to control every aspect of our lives. The restricted area became known as the ghetto and was divided into two parts, the "large ghetto" and the "small ghetto," which were separated by a main road, Paneriu Street, that ran through the area. A wooden bridge was built across the road so that we could get from one part of the ghetto to the other.

The ghetto was established in the oldest, poorest part of town, known by the Jews as Slobodka. About six thousand Jews and two thousand gentiles lived there before the war. The gentiles had to move out of the area while all the Jews of Kaunas, and some Jews from surrounding areas, had to move in. Approximately thirty thousand Jews were forced into an area where seven or eight thousand people had previously lived.

Families became frantic in the search for living space. My parents were desperate until they finally found a Lithuanian family willing to exchange their poor home in the small ghetto for our apartment in the city. We left them our furniture in exchange for their inferior possessions.

Only horse-drawn wagons and hand-pulled carts were allowed for moving our possessions. My father packed all our books in cartons and insisted we take them into the ghetto with us. This did not sit well with my mother, who wanted to take things other than books. But eventually all the cartons of books were stacked up in our cramped space in the ghetto.

Most houses in the ghetto were old single- or double-storey wooden homes without running water; instead there were wells and hand pumps in the yard. The toilets were in the yard, too. This required a huge adjustment to our way of life, but we could have lived with it if we had not been constantly harassed and threatened.

In our area, German soldiers went from house to house demanding that we hand over all valuables, jewellery, wedding rings, furs, cameras, silverware and musical instruments. All demands were preceded by a threat: "If you hide something and we find it, we will shoot you and everyone in the whole house." My parents gave up their wedding rings, silver candlesticks, a camera and my mother's fur and jewellery. I remember the soldiers making a list of the items they took from us. They wrote our name on top and even gave us a copy. They gave us a receipt for what they stole from us!

Some influential Lithuanians resented giving up their homes to Jews in the ghetto area and demanded their homes be returned to them. This was before the barbed wire fence was erected. The boundary of the ghetto was constantly changing, and we had to move out of the house we had arranged to live in. In fact, we moved many times while we were in the ghetto. Each time, we moved with fewer and fewer possessions. I remember lagging behind my parents and my uncles, carrying items from one place to another. In the end we had one room, which we had to share with a single woman who had been living there before we moved in. But we still had our books with us. It took a while for life in the ghetto to settle down.

The German authorities soon demanded that all Jewish men from age fifteen to fifty-five present themselves for work. Workers were required to be at the gate of the ghetto by six o'clock every morning. There they were formed into brigades and marched under guard to various work places. Some were building the airport; others were digging ditches, building roads, cleaning hospitals or working in factories. This was strenuous work, and it was slave labour — no pay. The workers were told that they were lucky to receive food in the ghetto. I was thirteen years old. I wasn't going to school, and I did not have to go to work. I had nothing to do.

~

As soon as the Jews of Kovno were driven into the ghetto, teachers from the wide network of Jewish schools in the city before the war began to talk about creating a school for children. The need was great, for there were children who had lost their parents during the early killings, and also some orphans from the Jewish orphanage of Kovno. My uncle Gedalie Wilentschuk, who was for many years the managing director of the Jewish orphanage, began to work with a committee to establish such a school. Gedalie was a prominent member of the community.

The committee had difficulty finding a place in the ghetto, but with some assistance from the Ältestenrat, the Jewish Council of Elders, a place was secured and the school began functioning. That contact brought my uncle Gedalie into the circle of the ghetto management, which later influenced our chances for survival.

When we lived in the small ghetto section, there were worrying rumours that the Germans were planning some kind of action. No one knew any details. One day in September 1941, a German officer, Captain Fritz Jordan, came to the Ältestenrat and gave them five thousand certificates bearing his name, instructing them to give these only to working tradespeople. When word spread about these documents, which were promptly called "Jordan Schein [certificate]," it was suspected that they might give some kind of protection.

I do not know how these certificates were being distributed, but I clearly remember a heated discussion between my uncles Tanchum and Gedalie, who, due to his access to the Jewish Council, had access to these certificates. He appeared very reluctant to go and ask for preferential treatment in obtaining these from the council, and his brother berated him for that, telling him that if he did not use his connections, as others would, he should resign from his position and make space for someone else to benefit. Eventually, Gedalie went and returned with four Jordan certificates. My father got one and each of my three uncles took one.

On October 4, 1941, we were awakened from our beds at about 6:00 in the morning by loud bangs on our doors and shouts of "Get out!" We dressed hurriedly and were told to go to a large square just outside the small ghetto. The barbed wire fence was opened at this point. Many German soldiers and Lithuanian guards were present. Some activity was going on near the two hospitals in our area. A heavy fog hung in the air and we could not see clearly. Then the soldiers demanded that anyone with Jordan certificates stand to one side. Our whole family moved over. After a while our group were driven out over the bridge to the large ghetto. We saw that the hospital of contagious diseases was surrounded with soldiers as we walked past it.

We went to the Knebels, my mother's half sister and her family, and they squeezed their family in and made space for all of us in one large room. We had arrived with no possessions whatsoever. We had nothing but the clothes on our backs.

The rest of the Jews from the small ghetto were taken to the Ninth Fort and murdered. They also took away the children from the orphanage and school in the small ghetto. Close to two thousand people were murdered that day.

Soon after we arrived in the large ghetto we saw fire where we had come from. The Germans had locked up the gates and doors to the contagious diseases hospital and set it on fire, with the patients, nurses and one doctor inside. I climbed up to a higher spot in the ghetto and watched the fire, thinking of what must have been going on inside.

We were later allowed to go back into the small ghetto and collect some belongings, carrying everything on our backs over the bridge. I also remember carrying books, hidden in bags of clothes.

⁓

Our family in the ghetto consisted of my mother, my father and my maternal grandmother, Alte, as well as my mother's three brothers, Tanchum, Gedalie and David, and David's wife, Miriam (Mary).

David and Mary had a baby girl, Shulamit, who was around five months old at the time.

Before moving into the ghetto, my uncle David had been a very successful and respected tailor in Kaunas. He had a distinguished clientele, including government ministers, and so had managed to save a good deal of money. He converted some of that money to Russian gold coins known as chervontzy. At some point between 1938 and 1939, the Lithuanian government had passed a law that no one was permitted to own gold. All gold had to be exchanged at the banks for paper money. Uncle David decided not to give up his gold; he placed the coins in a bag and hid it between two walls in his apartment. When the Germans forced us out of our homes, Uncle David, at significant risk, brought these coins with him into the ghetto.

At that point, our whole family was still living in a large wooden building in the small ghetto. Before the war, this building had housed the world-famous Slobodka yeshiva — a Jewish religious seminary for young men. The wooden building was old, without modern facilities. In the yard, there was a communal latrine with a long row of toilet seats over a deep cement hole.

When the order came from the Nazis to hand over all money, gold, silver, cameras, musical instruments, furs, jewellery, and in fact anything of value, my uncle David decided not to give his hard-earned gold to the Nazis. He sewed up twelve leather bags, each about three inches by eight inches, filled them with the gold coins and threw the bags of gold into the latrine. The latrine was full, and the bags immediately sank to the bottom.

When we had to leave the small ghetto, we moved out of that old seminary building and, as I mentioned, crossed the wooden footbridge into the large ghetto to live with our relatives the Knebel family. The nine of us — my three uncles, my aunt Mary, baby Shulamit, my grandmother and my parents and I — shared one large room.

The food supply to the ghetto was controlled by the Nazis, and less and less of it was being delivered to the Ältestenrat, whose job it was to distribute food to the inmates. The weekly food ration was hardly enough to sustain a normal person, and people who worked outside the ghetto risked a beating trying to buy food to smuggle back into the ghetto to their families.

We soon began to experience extreme hunger, but we realized that it was possible to buy additional food on the black market. Those who had hidden some money managed to bribe the Lithuanian police who were guarding the ghetto. Bread, butter, flour and even cattle were brought in secretly and slaughtered in the ghetto for kosher meat. And so, to avoid starvation, we began to think of how we could retrieve the gold my uncle David had thrown in the latrine. First, my uncle Gedalie signed himself up to join the work unit that cleaned the small ghetto area, which was now devoid of people. Luckily, he was assigned to clean the building of the yeshiva where we had lived. He was prepared: he had fitted a long stick with a bent nail at the end for a hook. The latrine had been emptied, and only a shallow layer of excrement remained at the bottom. Through a hole, he poked around with the stick until he was able to detect the leather bags with the gold, but he could not hook them on to the stick.

My uncle went looking for help. Luckily, he found the man whose job it was to empty the latrines; we called him "the Shmarravoz," a derogatory name that meant someone who was extremely dirty. Gedalie approached him and told him that there was gold in the latrine and asked if he would help get it out. "Do we share fifty/fifty?" the man asked. Uncle agreed. They returned to the latrine, and the Shmarravoz put on his long leather gloves, lowered himself into the hole and walked along the bottom, sliding along the floor in his tall boots. Soon he felt something on the ground, picked it up and asked my uncle, who was watching him through one of the toilet seats above, if that was what he was looking for. It was. He handed the bag to my uncle. The next bag he picked up, he put into his own large pocket. He picked up all twelve bags and gave six to my uncle, who placed them in his trouser and coat pockets, and kept six for himself.

By the time the Shmarravoz climbed out of the hole, the work day was over and it was time to go back to the large ghetto. My uncle was concerned about entering the gate, as the guards often searched the workers who were returning. "Don't worry about that. You just stay close to me and the wagon," said the Shmarravoz. On arriving at the gate, the man shouted to the German guards: "The 4711 brigade is coming!" (4711 is the name of a famous eau de cologne, a popular perfume still available today). It was the jokey way of saying that we were the stink brigade. All the guards held their noses and moved as far as possible from the wagon and the terrible smell. My uncle, the Shmarravoz and the horse-drawn wagon marched into the ghetto undisturbed!

I remember very clearly my uncle coming home and knocking on the window from outside. I saw my father open the window and ask, "What's this terrible smell?" "Don't ask, Julius, just come outside. I have the gold!" They washed the bags outside by the water pump, then cut them open and washed the coins several times. My father helped my uncle take off his clothes and burned them in a hole outside the house.

We had the gold! New bags of leather were sewn, and my father, who worked at the ghetto hospital, had the task of hiding the gold. He buried the six bags of gold under the foundation wall in the second basement of the hospital. Over time he took everyone, including me, to see the hiding place, in case one of us survived.

Once a month my father removed one coin and brought it to Uncle David. Uncle David had a contact who would buy the coin for a large pack of paper money, either German Reichsmark or Soviet rubles, as both currencies had value. This one gold coin per month fed our family of nine and the Knebel family of eight, plus other members of the wider family, including my aunt Mary's family.

I knew people who were hungry in the ghetto. Without the gold and the extra rations we were able to buy, it would have been very difficult to feed all the members of our family for those three years in the ghetto. We spent the money carefully, as we never knew how long we would be there and feared running out of gold. There was also the possibility of trying to escape from the ghetto to hide in a peasant's home somewhere, and that would be very costly.

We also placed one coin in the heel of one shoe of each member of the family, in case of sudden deportation. I believe we used up about a third of the gold coins during our three years in the ghetto. The rest remained under the foundation wall in the basement of the hospital, which was burned down after we left the ghetto in 1944.

~

On October 28, 1941, an announcement was posted that stated that no one was to go to work the next day. At six o'clock in the morning, everyone would have to gather in Demokratu Square, the large field in the middle of the ghetto. There were to be no exceptions — even children and those who were sick had to come to the field. Anyone found at home would be shot on the spot. No reason was given. "Leave the doors unlocked" were the instructions. My grandmother was very ill, and there was no way she could walk to the field, so we set her up with food and water and left her at home.

Early in the morning on October 29, twenty-six thousand people assembled on that field. We were told to gather in family units. At one end of the field stood SS Gestapo Master Sergeant Helmut Rauca. Families were instructed to approach him. He questioned the adults as to where they worked and who their family members were. He then directed families to go either to the right or to the left. The families on the left could return home; the families on the right had to gather outside the ghetto near the fence, where soldiers were guarding them.

The entire ghetto population was made to walk past Rauca. It took the whole day. We had no idea what was going on. At the end of the day, when our family approached, Rauca seemed uninterested in us; he just waved us away. It appeared he had his quota and needed no

more. I saw that the families who had gone to the right were surrounded by soldiers and sent to the small ghetto. We rushed home to
find my grandmother still in bed. No one had looked into our home.
Sadly, she died a few days later and was buried in the ghetto cemetery.

The morning after the selection by Rauca, we saw a large mass of
people being marched away from the ghetto toward the Ninth Fort
on the hill. The Ninth Fort was a large military compound surrounded by stone walls. That same day, all these men, women and children
— 9,200 people — were murdered, gunned down. Their bodies were
thrown into long trenches that had been dug beforehand by Russian
prisoners of war. The supervisors were Germans; the shooters were
Lithuanians. This tragic event was known as the Great Action.

The Nazis kept meticulous records of their crimes. The Jäger Report, a chilling document that was written by Karl Jäger, commandant of killing squad Einsatzkommando 3, records that on the day
of October 29, 2,007 men, 2,920 women and 4,273 children were
murdered, a total of 9,200. Reason for executions: "solving the Jewish
problem in Lithuania."[1]

The officer who oversaw this whole operation and made the selec-
tions — Helmut Rauca — later became well known to Canadians.
He entered Canada in 1950 and became a Canadian citizen in 1956.
Arrested in 1982, he was charged with 11,584 murders and was extradited to Germany for trial, becoming the first Canadian to be arrested
and extradited on war-crimes charges. Rauca died in prison at age
seventy-four, before his case came to trial.

∼

---

1   The Jäger Report is a nine-page document that tallied the number of murders in
Lithuania, Latvia and Belarus over a five-month period. From July to November
1941, the Nazis and their collaborators committed 137,346 murders of mostly Jewish citizens; in Kovno alone, 15,000 Jews were killed.

News, gossip and conversation in the ghetto were all about death. To avoid contemplating how I was going to die, I found activities to keep me occupied. In a small patch of earth in the yard, I planted some tomato and cucumber seeds. I didn't expect them to grow, but they did. Everyone mocked me, saying, "How long do you plan to be here in the ghetto?" I did not reply. Later, when I produced radishes, beautiful tomatoes and cucumbers, our neighbours living around the same yard became very jealous. They formed a committee and divided the "land" between us all, and I was left with a narrow strip by the fence. I had observed that cucumbers have thin tendrils that cling to anything, so I strung up rough string from the ground to the top of the fence and planted cucumbers at the bottom. Lo and behold, the cucumber plants climbed up the strings, and my cucumbers ripened while hanging in the air. I had very clean, perfect cucumbers.

At the end of the season, the neighbours watched me drying tomato seeds for planting next year. They were horrified and yelled at me, "You plan to be here another year?!" As if, by preparing to plant seeds for the following year, I was causing the continuation of our suffering in the ghetto.

But the next year spring we were still there, and I planted again, and so did all our neighbours, who begged me for some seeds. That fall they got furious when I began to collect seeds again! This time they were right — I never got to plant the seeds again.

Another activity that kept me occupied was looking for wood to burn to heat the house, and I would wander around the yards looking for anything that could burn. I carried a crude little saw that I hid under my jacket. I would go out at night with the woman with whom we shared our one room. She was a feisty woman who had been brought up in the Jewish orphanage and was much tougher than me. When we came upon a wooden picket fence, she would stand guard while I sawed the boards.

We weren't the only ones doing this, and there was not much to find. One night, however, we came across a fully intact white picket fence around a house. The house was dark and it was very quiet around. Carefully and quietly, I sawed through the top crossbar and the lower crossbar. I thought I had cut through the bars completely and could lift out the whole section without making noise, but the section would not move, so to free it I bent it downward, which caused a loud screech from the bottom boards breaking. In the dark, I didn't see that the bottom boards hadn't been sawn through.

Immediately a light in the house went on. People ran out, some in their underwear, screaming, "Thieves, thieves!" Suddenly a Jewish ghetto policeman was on the scene, and I took off. My partner remained there, pretending she was just passing by. The policeman ran after me. I fled toward a field with high bushes, hoping to dive in there, but the policeman, breathing heavily, was too close. He caught up with me, grabbed me by the arm and dragged me back to the scene of the crime. I told him, half sobbing, that I was not a thief and that I was just trying to take some wood from the fence. We came back to the house and he asked the owners what I had stolen from them. They were furious and shouted, "He cut down the fence!" The policeman let go of my arm and said, "That is not stealing!" He walked away.

By this time there were more people around, and my partner shouted, "That poor kid just wanted some firewood and they accused him of stealing." Then the whole crowd began to break up the fence. Even the owners came out with saws then, trying to save some wood for themselves. Within a half hour there was no fence whatsoever! My partner urged me to grab some wood too, but I was too upset, so she was left to bring a few sticks home on her own. The ghetto had its own rules and its own morality. I had to wonder what had happened to me.

～

As I mentioned, we were forbidden to own anything of value. My parents had already turned in their wedding rings, jewellery, silver candlesticks, watches and cameras. We were forbidden to read newspapers and own radios. Then we heard they were coming for our books. The order from the Nazis came on February 27, 1942: "Hand over your books." Like all the other orders, the book *Aktion* came with the threat that disobedience meant death.

My father was heartbroken that he had to give up his beloved books. He had insisted on bringing all our books into the ghetto, and we had carted them from place to place. When the time came to hand them over, he selected some of his less favourite books and stacked them in a wheelbarrow. Then he and I went to deliver the books to the synagogue, which was the designated collection centre. When we arrived at the synagogue with our wheelbarrow full of books, an amazing sight greeted us: the benches had been removed, and the small room was filling up with a mountain of books, reaching from the entrance almost up to the balcony at the back, which was the women's section. People were walking over books, falling over books and kept coming to drop off more books.

My father surveyed this sad scene and remarked to me that the Germans had posted no guards. "They trust us with the books!" he exclaimed. Then he looked down and noticed some books that were nicely bound in red cloth. "Look at this — all ten books of the Pushkin collection of 1937. I wanted to buy them last year, but could not afford it." Pushkin, the greatest Russian poet, died in 1837, and in 1937 an anniversary edition of all his poetry was published. So, there was my father holding in his hands the ten books of the deluxe edition of the greatest poet of the Russian language.

My father turned to me and said, "Elly, take out the books we brought and leave them on the pile, then put these in the wheelbarrow — we will take them home." He bent down again and picked up two volumes of *History of the Jews* in German, by Graetz. "Put these in the wheelbarrow, too," he said. "It is a fine set." Looking further, he picked out the books he wanted. Now the wheelbarrow was full, so we covered it with a newspaper and went home.

And we did the trip seven times — going with an empty wheelbarrow, coming back with a full one!

My mother was afraid and angry. "What are you doing? You want them to come and kill us all?"

"Don't worry," said my father, "we won't keep them in the house."

Now we had a whole new collection of books, which we had to hide. In the yard of the house where we lived there was a large garden shed. I climbed into the attic space above the boarded ceiling, and my father handed me all the books. It was dark there, so to get light I lifted out a clay tile or two from the roof above. Over the next few days I spent all my time up there in the shed, and with boards and bricks I sorted out the books and built book shelves. I had a great library!

Although there was no school for me, I spent a lot of time reading world literature. I taught myself Russian quite well by reading and memorizing Pushkin's poetry, which I really loved. I read the Russian classics — Tolstoy, Lermontov, the greats. I read the German classics, too. I worked through Goethe's *Faust* — an effort like reading (much later) Milton's *Paradise Lost* in English. That was my education in the ghetto.

The fate of those books was the same as the fate of the Jews. When the time came to evacuate the last of the Jews, all the buildings in the ghetto were set ablaze and burned down.

Treasures and Transformations

With the adults at work all day, the remaining youth were left without supervision and were running wild. Some enlightened leaders in the ghetto realized that to save the children they had to get them off the streets.

In the summer of 1942, the Ältestenrat requested permission from the Nazis to establish a vocational school for children aged twelve to fifteen. The elders said that they would train the youngsters to be useful for the war effort. Permission was granted by the Nazis. Before the war, Kaunas had a well-known Jewish trade school run by the ORT. Many of the staff and teachers from the school were now in the ghetto. Jacob Oleiski, who was the previous director of ORT Kaunas, became the director of the proposed ghetto training school, the Fachschule.

A notice appeared at the Ältestenrat that they were going to open a school to teach boys locksmithing and metal work, carpentry, woodwork and bricklaying; girls would be taught sewing. I was among the first boys to volunteer to learn locksmithing. When I arrived the first morning I found a teacher, but no school. Although the Germans had given permission to go ahead with the school, there was absolutely no equipment provided.

The teacher, Yerachmiel Feldman, was a skilled instructor from the Kaunas ORT School. He announced to the few boys who showed up that he would teach us locksmithing and metal work, but that we first needed to find tools and build the school. He suggested that we go to the basements of old houses and look for tools of any kind, no matter how rusted or damaged they were. He said we should also bring back any old metal bedsteads that were made of solid iron. The newer ones were made of metal pipes and were not suitable for us.

We were disappointed that there was no real school, but we went to work scavenging in the ghetto. To our surprise, we very soon discovered treasure. The ghetto, as I mentioned, was in the oldest, most impoverished Jewish section of the city. Before the war, the area had housed workshops and small manufacturing places of all kinds. Now that people were crowded into every available room, they had thrown out anything that used to fill the rooms. Tools and drill stands, scrap metal, old beds and old motors were simply dumped in the crawl spaces under the floors. We explored these dark spaces and ran back to Mr. Feldman in triumph when we found something.

After more than a week of this activity, our group of potential students had grown. With the energy and enthusiasm of youth we had collected a huge pile of every kind of metal, tool and machinery part. Feldman was the king of the heap. When we brought something that we thought looked like garbage, he encouraged us by saying, "That will be very useful! Wait till we clean it up. You'll see."

Feldman then sent us out to an abandoned building to pick up wooden boards so that we could build workbenches. A saw materialized from somewhere, and soon we had built several very sturdy benches. Some were longer than others, depending on the wood we could find, but all were the same height and width. We lined them up in one spacious room in two rows.

To our considerable surprise, Feldman pulled out vices from the junk pile. Covered in dirt and rust, we had not recognized them as essential pieces of equipment. Each boy was given one vice, a cloth, a can of paraffin and a piece of sandpaper. After we cleaned the vices with the paraffin from the outside, we had to take them apart and clean the threads and the inside of the jaws. We used bits of metal to scratch away layers of grime from every corner and crevice, our hands and arms turning black with dirt and old grease. After years of forgotten slumber, the vices began to look like working tools again. We mounted them on the benches about one yard apart, and we now had workstations. Feldman examined the work and distributed praise carefully, never giving a false compliment; criticism was specific, measured, without malice.

"Now, boys, you need to find tools that look like this." Feldman held up a hacksaw. We turned the pile we had collected upside down, and to our amazement, we saw dozens of hacksaws — old, rusted, full of earth and dirt. So back to cleaning we went. Paraffin to wash off the dirt and grease, then we took them apart to sand and clean. Some had the wooden handle missing, and others were bent out of shape, so we cannibalized the parts and fitted up a respectable number of complete hacksaws. Feldman somehow got a collection of hacksaw blades, and we now had twenty "new" hacksaws, ready to cut metal.

The next search was for metal files. Feldman showed us how to differentiate between a rough, coarse file, called a "bastard" (I did not know the meaning of this term in English — it came as a major surprise to me years later, after I learned the language) and a medium file with finer teeth. As we had picked up anything that looked like metal, we were pleased to find that we had brought in a sizable number of files. Slowly we cleaned them up and added wooden handles that were retrieved from other files. A wire brush was used to clean up the files well, as a file won't work when the grooves are filled with dirt. We learned that the best files were marked "Sheffield Made in England."

In the pile were little metal instruments that looked like a horse's head. Rusted, they seemed useless, but lovingly cleaned up and carefully oiled, they became calipers, now gleaming and perfectly useful for measuring. We did the same with metal right angles, and we had enough of them for a few on every workbench.

After a few weeks of these preparations we were nearly ready to start, but we still needed a drilling machine and a grindstone. After Feldman explained what they looked like, we were sent out again to scavenge. This time we knew the ghetto area better, so we began searching the places that looked like they had been workshops at one time. We found a drill that was so heavy that we had to call for reinforcements. We dragged this clumsy, old, cast-iron, floor model drill press to our school, where it took a few days to get the clunker back into a presentable form. Feldman tightened the bearings with a few tricks we did not understand and declared himself satisfied. A motor with a grindstone at each end was also found, but the grindstones were misshapen. We built a wooden stand and mounted the grinder on top of it, and then Feldman showed us how to shape the grindstones by carefully wearing away the uneven surfaces.

Useful items like drill bits, files, calipers, metal rulers and scraping needles began clandestinely to show up in our school. Jews working in official workshops that had been set up in the ghetto to serve the needs of the German authorities were supplying us. Everything was a treasure.

Imitating Feldman, we all tried to find a rough shirt with a chest pocket that had a narrow part sewn off at one side to hold a caliper. To walk around with your own caliper stuck in that narrow slot was a source of immense pride, and I asked my mother to sew a vertical seam in my shirt pocket. Feldman had a Mauser caliper of his own, from the same German company that made the famous Mauser pistols and rifles. I still have a Mauser caliper in my workshop that I obtained after the war, which I cherish.

Now the classes began. Our first task was to learn to file a cube out of the pieces of rusted iron we had cut from the old bed frames. Guiding a file in a flat path is a difficult skill that takes several months to master. At first, when we filed the metal piece and looked through a rectangle frame to see how flat the piece was, we saw a curved mountain. Feldman regularly took a student's file and demonstrated the rhythmic movement of hands and body needed to guide the file forward with pressure and back with a free slide. It looked so simple, but we could not do it!

My friend Yankele tried jamming the file between his stomach and the bench and sliding the metal piece on it to get a flat surface. Feldman noticed this, took a hammer and smashed the metal on an anvil. Yankele had to cut a new piece and start from scratch. Eventually most of us learned to produce a cube with flat, right-angled sides. My view of iron as a hard, unmanageable material changed — I started see it as malleable and transformable. I loved the power I had to shape and form it, and the pleasure in doing it successfully remained with me for life.

A special challenge was to use a hammer and chisel the way Feldman did. He would hold the chisel with three fingers over the metal and hit the hammer hard on top of the chisel. The challenge was to hit the chisel with a two-pound hammer without looking at the head of the chisel. My eyes had to be on the working surface, where the cutting edge of the chisel was hitting the metal. If I missed the head of the chisel, the hammer came down hard on my fingers. I was determined to learn, so I wounded myself many times till I got it right. That skill has remained with me to this day. I know where the hammer will come down, without looking at its trajectory.

Feldman was a man of few words and a wonderful teacher. He would demonstrate the correct technique again and again, then walk away to let us practice on our own. Later, he would inspect our progress.

After about six months studying the mechanical skills of shaping metal, we began learning locksmithing, and the fascinating world of lock construction was opened to us. We learned about repairing all kinds of locks, fitting springs, making keys; we designed our own locks, making every part from those old iron bedsteads and polishing them to a mirror finish.

We had an exhibition of our work and the Nazi officers came to inspect it. I was proud that one officer pointed to my shiny, handmade padlock, but then very unhappy when he said he wanted it and took it away. To add insult to injury, I had to make him a second key!

I remember the day Feldman brought in an old lathe. We worked for a week cleaning it and setting it up with a motor and a belt drive. Now we could learn to operate a lathe. It was exciting to see what new forms we could shape. Everyone took turns learning the finer points of operating the lathe — cutting threads of precise dimensions and nuts to fit them.

Working with metals fascinated me. Eventually I came to feel that each metal had a "taste" of its own: the bite of the file into steel felt different than it did for brass or copper — I could recognize each metal blindfolded. When drilling into steel, oil was useful to assist the drill bit to drive faster, but for aluminum, oil did not help at all.

All this activity took place amidst the most appalling conditions of ghetto life. Our survival was always in question. From day to day we did not know who would come back to school; from time to time, boys just disappeared, their fates unknown. Being in school took our minds away from thoughts of impending doom, from our fear for tomorrow.

Even in this desperate situation, the leaders insisted that we study Jewish subjects. We discussed history and we played chess. We even put on a play by I.L. Peretz.[2] As I look back, I must give credit to those dedicated and inspired teachers. Life in the ghetto was miserable, and the school was a place of respite.

One part of the training that no one liked was blacksmithing. It wasn't that we didn't like the work — it was the teacher. I think we called him Yosef the blacksmith. He was old, grumpy and impatient, and the shed where he worked was dark, dirty and smoky. Yosef was short and somewhat bent over. He did not speak to students on prin-

---

2 The play, *Mekubolim*, was performed at a special festive concert dedicated to the one-year anniversary of the school and took place on July 3, 1943.

ciple — when he was trained as an apprentice, the master craftsman had not spoken to him either. But everyone knew that Yosef was a genius with iron. With the most primitive equipment he could make anything, from a multi-leaf spring for a car to a delicate clasp for a door.

When my turn came to go to his workshop, I went with some trepidation. I walked in and he immediately turned his back to me. Facing the forge, he turned up the blower to fan the flames then picked up a piece of steel about six inches long with large pliers that were suspended from the ceiling on a wire. He pushed one end of the steel into the fire and waited. I stood there waiting for something to happen. After a while the end of the piece of steel became red hot. He pulled it out of the fire and placed the hot end on the anvil while holding it with the long pliers. Then he picked up a small hammer and softly hit the hot end of the steel bar. He looked at me and I looked back. He gave a loud grunt and pointed with his head to a ten-kilogram hammer in the corner. I got the hint and picked up the large hammer. Again, he hit the steel with his little hammer and looked up at me with his bloodshot eyes. I got it! He wanted me to hit the steel where he was pointing with his little hammer! So, I lifted the large hammer over my head and came down hard on the hot steel. Instead of a bang, it made a soft sound, like hitting stiff rubber, but the steel showed a flat spot where I had hit it. He turned the steel over and again hit the end with his hammer. I came down hard with my hammer. The steel now began to look like a chisel and I realized what we were producing.

The work began to go smoothly. He tapped with the little hammer; I banged down with the big one at the spot he indicated. He smoothly controlled the shape of the steel piece; I delivered the blows that formed it. I felt happy; all was going well, like the Anvil Chorus in the opera "Gypsy Baron." Then he hit the metal twice. I came down with the big hammer and the steel went flying across the workshop.

Now he talked! He cursed me in Yiddish, Russian, Polish and several other languages, I think — words and curses I had never heard before. That was also an education for me.

Apparently in blacksmith language one hit means go and two hits means stop. But a master does not talk to an apprentice, a species regarded as lower than the earth. Finally, when Yosef ran out of curses, he picked up the cooled steel from the floor and put it back in the forge. We eventually finished making the chisel. When it was completed, he dipped the tip in cold water, which hissed from contact with the red-hot metal. He withdrew it, and I watched the colours change from orange to yellow to blue. Then he dropped the whole piece into the water. This process hardens the end of the chisel so it can cut into metal without blunting.

I decided there and then that I was going to learn from him, no matter how he tried to put me off. Once I got mad at him and shouted, "Talk to me, don't grunt!" To my surprise, he began talking to me. He said he could see that I really wanted to learn, not like those other… (I won't repeat what he called my fellow students).

My admiration for Yosef's skill knew no bounds. He was a craftsman of the highest level. I loved the harmony of his movements. The other boys complained about him and the dark, sooty place where we had to work, and I told them how I enjoyed the process of lifting the hammer, aiming and then connecting with the steel, how it sounded to me like: Piff-Puff-Poi — lift the heavy hammer, BOOM — hit the metal, then Chick-Chuck — the double echo of the hit.

I've had a number of nicknames in my life, but "Piff-Puff-Poi BOOM-Chick-Chuck" was one of the strangest. For the remainder of the time we were in the ghetto that was my name in the school: Piff-Puff-Poi BOOM-Chick-Chuck. The students were not lazy — they did not mind the time it took to say it all — every time! Later, when I became a teacher, they still said it, but behind my back.

The skills I learnt from my teachers Feldman and Yosef the blacksmith would later save both my life and my father's. But at the time, while we were still in the ghetto, I was just happy to make a little money for myself by using what I'd learnt.

One area of business that showed promise was fixing sewing machines to sell to farmers in exchange for food. The farmers wanted only Singer sewing machines. If anyone had a different make, like a Pfaff sewing machine, there were artists in the ghetto who could paint the Singer logo over the Pfaff logo with gold paint. My job was to repair the broken parts or create replacement parts. Once, I had to produce a spindle for a sewing machine foot drive — a delicate part. I did not know how to bend the steel shaft for the eccentric drive, so I went to my blacksmith friend. I was amazed at his dexterity. I later mounted his shaped steel in the lathe, and it ran true, with no wobble — it was perfect!

I also learnt how to open a Yale lock without a key. When people lost their keys and could not get into their homes, I was the one they called. I received either money or some food for this service. People always wanted to know how I did it, but this was my professional secret. I am grateful to Feldman, who not only taught me to be a locksmith but also showed me the beauty of various lock mechanisms and designs. To this day I am fascinated by locks and the part they have played in the history of civilization. The ancient Egyptians had wooden locks and keys that closely resemble our modern Yale locks, except they were much larger.

I developed another little side business in the ghetto. I discovered that it was possible to heat water in a glass or pot very quickly by inserting two electrodes in the water and plugging them in to electricity. I began to produce these "heaters" and sell them. My heaters became popular because they were well made and did not cause shocks to the user, as rougher models did. In any case, they were very dangerous appliances. One could easily get electrocuted by touching the bare electrodes while they were plugged in, but these were tough times and one had to use whatever was available.

~

Like everyone else in the ghetto, when students in our school turned fifteen, they had to present themselves for a slave labour work detail (later on, the minimum age for slave labour duty was lowered to twelve). Due to the training they had received at the school, some of them got good jobs either inside or outside the ghetto in the workshops that produced items for the war effort. The opportunity to work in a factory was in many cases a lifesaver, as it enabled people to obtain food while outside the ghetto. And the work was easier than digging trenches or building roads.

In March 1943, when I turned fifteen, the school offered me the opportunity to become an assistant instructor. I don't know what went on behind the scenes or how the school management got me excused from slave labour, but I was very happy to become a teacher. Feldman was the model for my teaching style — not Yosef the blacksmith!

The school had grown and there were more students. Soon I got to be a full instructor, with morning and afternoon classes of my own. The students were secretly amused by my enthusiasm for the subjects, but most did their best to learn. I had some odd students. One was a medical doctor who decided he wanted to learn metalwork. He was very diligent, worked hard and soon became quite skilled. Once, he produced a tap holder, a somewhat complicated tool to hold a tap for cutting threads in a metal hole. He was very proud of it and showed it to all his doctor friends. Teacher Feldman's dry comment was, "He is a doctor amongst metal workers and a metal worker amongst doctors!"

We had several classes alternating between mornings and afternoons. We taught the theory of metals, engineering drawing and some clandestine cultural classes on Hebrew and Jewish history, which were forbidden by the Germans.

All these activities allowed me to direct my mind away from the one thought that floated in my head during the three years in the ghetto: How will I die? I imagined being shot and thrown — still alive — into a trench with dead bodies on top of me. Buried alive.

One day in 1944, a Jewish man I did not know appeared in the school. He opened his leather jacket and pointed his camera at me while I worked at the bench with a few students. A click, and he was gone. Cameras were forbidden to us in the ghetto. If he had been caught, he would have been executed immediately. I later learned that the brave photographer's name was George Kadish, known in the ghetto as Hirsch Kadushin. Exactly fifty years later, in May 1994, I was astonished to find a copy of this photograph in the United States Holocaust Memorial Museum in Washington, DC.[3]

---

3   The photo can be found on page 161. Elly now shows this photo to students when he is invited to schools to tell his story.

Saving Shulamit

Another task I had was to look after my little cousin Shulamit. With all the adults busy and working morning to night, and her mother cooking for a whole family, I was the one who could spend time with her. I fed her, took her for walks, played with her, told her stories and watched her develop. It felt like she was my baby, and I loved her very much. She was speaking well at a very early age, and I was delighted to hear her learn new words so fast. She was always happy being with me and would run into my arms to greet me when I came in.

In 1943, as conditions in the ghetto worsened and survival, especially for the children, was even less assured, my uncle David and my aunt Mary decided to seek a way to get Shulamit out of the ghetto. Uncle David, as I mentioned, was an expert tailor, and his clients before the war were well connected. He secretly sent a letter to a friend, a fine Lithuanian man named Jonas Jablonskis who was a writer and intellectual, and asked if he would be willing to take his child. This action would have been punishable by death if discovered by the German authorities.

After a few days had passed, a letter was delivered to Uncle David from Jonas Jablonskis' wife, Jadvyga. She wrote that her husband had been arrested by the Soviets before the Germans occupied Lithuania, and she did not know whether he was alive or dead. She had no children and was willing to take Shulamit. My uncle arranged to meet her secretly at his place of work in the city and offered her money for the upkeep of his child. Jadvyga refused to take any payment; she wanted only the child. She did make one stipulation: she would return the child only to her parents — not to any other family member — if they survived the war.

With great secrecy, arrangements were made to deliver Shulamit to Jadvyga. It was a long walk from the ghetto to my uncle's workplace in the city, and the brigade he was in would stop on the way for a short rest under a bunch of trees. One morning in the summer of 1943, my mother gave two-and-a half-year-old Shulamit an anesthetic injection, which put her into a deep sleep. Uncle David placed her in a backpack and left for work with his brigade, under guard, as usual. When they arrived at the rest stop, he left the backpack with his daughter inside it under a tree and marched away with the group. He turned back and saw someone come and take the bag away, as had been arranged.

Later we received a message: "The goods have arrived." Shulamit was safe. I can't imagine what my uncle and aunt were going through, but I know how I felt. I didn't understand it at the time, but I think I fell into a depression. I missed her so much, and I lost the will to do anything. I was constantly thinking about how she woke up from the anesthetic among people she did not know, who spoke a language she did not understand. We spoke to her only in Yiddish, and Jadvyga spoke Lithuanian. I thought of the pain my little girl was experiencing, and my heart was sore. Her adoptive mother gave her a new name, Dalia, which in Lithuanian means fate.

On March 27, 1944, while most of the adults were out of the ghetto working, German soldiers arrived with trucks and buses and began a hunt for children and the elderly. This horrible event came to be known as the *Kinderaktion*, the children's action. Loud and lively music blared from the trucks while babies were torn from the arms of their mothers and thrown into the trucks and buses. Some mothers would not be separated from their children and went together with them to the buses. None of the kids under age twelve who were found hiding in basements, barrels and behind curtains were spared. Approximately one thousand children, along with hundreds of the elderly and sick, were either taken and murdered that day or deported to Auschwitz. The anguish and the wailing that went on in the ghetto when the parents came home from work and saw that their children were gone — I cannot describe it. I was relieved that our Shulamit had been smuggled out of the ghetto.

The brave woman who saved Shulamit/Dalia was Jadvyga (née Žakevičiute) Jablonskienė of Kaunas, Lithuania. In 2000, after our efforts to honour her name, Yad Vashem in Israel recognized her as Righteous Among the Nations for saving a Jewish child. The following is Dalia's story, as written by her.

Dalia's Story[4]

I woke up among strangers talking a strange language. The only words I knew were Yiddish. My name was Shulamit, but they called me Dalia, and that became my name. I can't tell you what I felt. I was only two years old. Lithuanian became my new language. The woman I now called Mother was young, blonde and beautiful. Grandmother was kind and good. I was a child and I didn't question anything. For three years I lived and played like a child, and I was happy in the way children are happy.

That all changed the day soldiers came to take away my mother. She was fighting, I was screaming and kicking and Grandmother was crying. I didn't know then that these were Russian soldiers. They had come to arrest my mother because they found out that she was writing and distributing leaflets. She was a Lithuanian nationalist and was fighting for the freedom of her country from the new communist occupiers after the war.

---

4 Written by Dalia Jackbo.

My mother was taken to a prison, where she was starving. Every day, Grandmother went there to bring her food. She couldn't look after both my mother and me, so she took me to live with another Lithuanian family. I knew them; they were my cousins. They had a big house and a yard with chickens. But I missed my mother and my grandmother.

One ordinary day my aunt called me to her and said my mother had come for me. I was very excited, but my mother wasn't there. Instead I saw a little grey-haired woman with a crippled hand. She wanted to hold me and kiss me. I screamed, "You're not my mother and you mustn't touch me!" She spoke to me in Yiddish and I told her, "Don't speak that language, they will kill you." My aunt told me that my grandmother was very ill and my beautiful mother was dead, that this woman was my real mother and I had to go with her.

I was five years old. [5]

---

5 For more details on Dalia's story and the fate of her adoptive mother, see http://db.yadvashem.org/righteous/family.html?language=en&itemId=4015374

Dachau

In the fall of 1943, the Kovno ghetto was transformed into a concentration camp. Dealing with the SS made everyone's lives much, much worse — many people were deported to Estonia and to newly created labour camps. Nonetheless, our family managed to stay in the Kovno ghetto. I worked in the trade school up to the very end, until the liquidation of the ghetto in the summer of 1944.

By June of 1944, the Soviet army had managed to drive the German army out of most of the Soviet Union. The front was now getting closer to our city. The remaining Jews in the ghetto — from the initial population of close to 30,000, we had been reduced to around 7,000 — were very anxious about what the Nazis would do when the Soviet front got to Kaunas.

On July 8, 1944, the announcement came: the Nazis were going to liquidate the ghetto and we were going to be transported elsewhere to work. We did not believe them. We were certain that before giving up the territory to the Soviet army, they would march us to the Ninth Fort and kill us, like they had done with thousands of others.

My fear of being shot, thrown into a trench and buried alive with dead bodies on top of me became a real possibility. A few prisoners who had escaped from the Ninth Fort had described such horrific events. That was the moment our family decided that we would not go. We would rather commit suicide. We found an empty room in the cement basement of a house and covered the entrance with a cupboard, as I described earlier.

As we waited, debating whether to end our lives, days passed. On the third morning, we heard the footsteps of two soldiers coming down the stairs into the basement. My mother picked up the first syringe. I had my arm bare and ready. But the soldiers walked past our covered door, went to the end of the passage and kicked in the coal shed door, and then opened the door opposite ours and said, "There is no one here." We heard the soldiers leave. My mother put the syringe back on the tray.

We sat in that basement for two or three more days, but we heard nothing more and began speculating. Perhaps the Soviet army had arrived and we were already free? We carefully pushed away the cupboard and went outside. The German guards were still there. We saw our people marching to a train. They didn't need a train to take us to be shot and killed at the Ninth Fort. Perhaps the Germans were not lying to us this time; perhaps they really were taking us somewhere to work. So, on July 12 or 13, 1944, we picked up the little packages we kept ready in case of a sudden deportation, and we went to the train.

We know now that after our train left, the Nazis went searching from house to house, setting each on fire. With the exception of the Ältestenrat building, not one house in the ghetto was spared. Many people had been hiding in basements, like we had. When the fires started they had to come out, and they were shot on the spot, or they were burned inside their hiding places. Our family would surely have died in the fire had we stayed another two days in the basement room.

～

I have terrible memories of trains.

When the concentration camp in Kaunas was liquidated, the train waiting for us at the station was not a passenger train, but a cattle train. By the time we got to the train, the wagon was already crowded.

When we thought the wagon was already packed to capacity, the Nazis pushed in another fifty people. Eventually, there were about two hundred people in the wagon. It was impossible to find a place to sit. We had no water, no toilet facilities and very little air. People became sick. Some people tried to jump out through the small window in the wagon, but most were immediately shot by soldiers riding at the end of the train. Others, we later found out, survived the jump.

Through the cracks in the wooden slats, we recognized that we were heading toward the border of Poland, in the direction of Germany. The following afternoon we arrived in Stutthof, a town in Germany close to the Polish border, and also close to a concentration camp by the same name. The doors to the wagon opened and we were ordered to get out and to push out the bodies of those who had died during the night. On the platform, the Germans separated the men from the women. It probably took only ten minutes. My father, my uncles and I were sent back onto the train. My mother and aunt remained on the platform.

The train took off again. We still had no water or food. We travelled for what felt like a long day and night, maybe two. I lost sense of time. We passed through Munich and stopped at a small station called Kaufering, in Bavaria. Under guard, we were marched off into the countryside. We arrived at a field surrounded by two rows of a barbed wire fence. There were watchtowers high up in the corners of the field. I remember seeing a sign on the gate that read: "K.L. Dachau Lager I." [Concentration Camp Dachau Camp I] It was July 15, 1944.

Dachau. We were all shaking with dread. Dachau was a name known and feared all over Europe. It was the first concentration camp Hitler established when he came to power in 1933, using it to lock up his political enemies: labour leaders, politicians, ministers of religion, newspaper publishers, editors and Jews.

The field was filled with simple huts. Could this be Dachau? It looked so primitive; we couldn't believe that this was the infamous concentration camp. We soon realized that we were not in the main camp but in a subcamp of the Dachau camp system, one of eleven such working camps around the Kaufering area.

A commandant, who we would soon find out was a vicious man, cursed us and yelled at us. The Nazis demanded that we hand over all the money and valuables that we had on us, and any possessions we brought with us were confiscated immediately. Some men went to the latrine — a makeshift structure over a trench in the ground — and threw in their paper money, rubles or other currency in a measure of defiance. The Nazis found out when currency began floating in the latrine. The commandant ordered four men to undress and forced them to wade into the latrine trench and fish out the currency with their hands. They then had to wash the money and lay it out on the grass to dry. After that, the commandant gave an order to burn the paper money.

Several wild-eyed, emaciated prisoners in striped uniforms arrived and began to cut and shave off our hair. Then the same barbers went about shaving our body hair. I was a shy sixteen-year-old and refused their demands — I shaved myself. So did my father.

Our shoes were the only items we could keep. Our own clothes were replaced with blue-and-white striped uniforms and matching caps. Each jacket had a number sewn on the left top pocket. My father got number 51,819, and I got 51,820.

We were each given an aluminum dish and a spoon and sent to the kitchen area to receive our first meal — a bowl of soup and a slice of bread. After that, in the open field, we were lined up in rows of five and counted. We were each given one blanket and sent off to the barracks, which at that time were temporary structures made of thin pressboard. Later those huts were replaced by more permanent barracks consisting of two long, flat, wooden surfaces that joined at an angle to make a pointed A-shaped roof. A trench was dug through the centre of the structure, and boards were placed on each side of the trench. We slept on the hard, horizontal boards, twenty-five men on each side. Soil was thrown over the roof, which in time sprouted grass, as insulation.

The first morning in Dachau we were woken at 6:00 a.m. by the sharp sound of a whistle. We were instructed to line up at the kitchen for coffee, which turned out to be a tepid brown liquid without sugar. Then we were sent back to the parade ground to be lined up and counted before being marched out to work under SS guard. We were not told what work we would be doing.

After marching for some time, we arrived at an immense construction site. It appeared to be a huge sand mountain about half a kilometre long that was being covered with cement and steel rods. What could they be building there? Why would they cover a sand mountain with concrete? At the front end of this construction there were bulldozers digging out the sand from inside the mountain where the concrete cover had been completed. It looked as if they were building a giant tunnel in the middle of the countryside.

There was some confusion deciding where each prisoner should go to work. There was a shout out for mechanics, woodworkers and blacksmiths. I raised my hand as a mechanic. Together with a few others, I was told to follow some German civilians. Four of us were selected by one of these civilians, and we were led to a three-storey wooden building.

We later realized that there were three such buildings. Each building contained four huge pumping machines. On the third floor, there were large mixers being filled with sand, small stones and cement. These materials arrived by train and were transferred separately by conveyers to the mixers. Steel arms stirred the containers while water was fed into them. Once properly stirred, the concrete mixture was emptied into an open conical container on the second floor. The tip of this container protruded through the floor into the top of the pump on the ground floor. In our building, there were four such set-ups feeding four pumps. The noise generated by these mixers and pumps was thunderous. To be heard over the roar of the pumps I had to shout in a high-pitched voice. In fact, I damaged my vocal chords working there.

I found that these giant pumps were driven by 150 horsepower electric motors. A reciprocating piston pushed a load of mixed concrete into a steel pipe that protruded through the wall outward. Three-metre-long steel pipes were joined together all the way to the building site, a distance that could be from one hundred metres up to one kilometre away. All the pipes were joined with hinged clamps, so they could be easily disconnected should they become blocked.

I was always curious about anything I saw, so one day, while marching to work, I asked the SS guard walking beside me, "What will this building be?" Before he could answer, my fellow prisoners berated me, hissing, "Are you crazy, asking such questions? They could shoot you as a spy!" The guard, seeing their worried expressions, said softly, "It will be a potato cellar." But I was certain that the construction had a military purpose.

It sure did have a military purpose! After the war, I found out all the details. Germany was the first country to develop a jet fighter plane, the Messerschmitt Me 262. It had a maximum speed of nine hundred kilometres per hour, way faster that any Allied fighter plane. The Me 262 was a formidable danger to the Allied bombers that were flying over Germany destroying factories and cities. Germany's problem was that they could not build the planes in sufficient numbers due to the constant bombing and destruction of the factories by the Allies. The German armaments industry was seeking a way to build these planes in a factory that was bomb-proof.

By this point in 1944, the war was going badly for Germany. Hitler was trying to reverse the progress of the Allies and agreed to the idea of constructing safe production facilities for the fighter planes. A civil engineer named Franz Xaver Dorsch was in charge of the construction. The idea was to pile up a mountain of sand about four hundred metres long and use it as a support for a curved tunnel of cast concrete reinforced by steel so thick that no known bomb could penetrate it. The shell was close to five metres thick. After the concrete shell was poured the sand had to be removed from the inside. The interior was the height of a four-storey building. This factory was to be part of a larger network of factories where the Germans planned to mass-produce the fighter planes. Thankfully, the construction of the factory was never completed when the war ended in total defeat for Germany. I am happy to report that I did not contribute to the German war effort, although I took an active part in building the massive facility.

The German supervisor of our liquid cement pumping station, whom we called *Meister* (master), explained to the four of us assigned to him how the pump worked. Its role was to transfer cement to the roof of the bunker. One problem that occurred regularly was that a stone would jam the piston, which pushed the concrete through the steel pipes. Then swift action was required to throw the clutch lever and stop the pump. Our job was then to dismantle the front end of the pump as quickly as possible, clean out the stuck cement, replace the stiff rubber ring on the piston and reassemble the machine. Time was of the essence, since the concrete in the cone above our pump could start hardening within a half hour. If a longer period was required to repair the pump, then complicated procedures had to be executed to clear out the cement in the system above us. Other prisoners were brought in to quickly clean away the cement before it would harden. The pumping was not to stop — construction went on twenty-four hours a day, seven days a week. The pump had to be maintained continuously, making sure oil always flowed to every bearing.

I learned the details of the job quickly. One day an oil feeder unit broke. There was no replacement, and I offered to repair it. The Meister was dubious that it could be repaired. I knew that I needed to drill a very small hole in the new shaft. Our workshop did not have the required size of drill bit, so I asked for a larger drill bit, ground it down to the required size and drilled the little hole. Then I repaired the pump. The Meister was impressed with my skill. After that incident, he started slipping me parts of his sandwiches and other food. He knew that we were starving. Food was the most valuable commodity in the camp.

While I was repairing the oil feeder, a German civilian engineer who oversaw the workshop was observing me and he asked me where I learned my skills. He said that in Germany all Jews were either bankers or lawyers. While this wasn't true, I assured him that in Lithuania many Jews were skilled craftsmen in electrical and mechanical trades, even blacksmithing.

The skills I learnt in the ghetto trade school helped me on many occasions. Once, the large metal buckle on the belt belonging to the Meister broke in half, and he was very upset because it would be impossible for him to find a replacement. When I took it from him and repaired it, he was delighted and unable to even detect how I did it. He rewarded me with half a loaf of bread and other food. My fine mechanical skills had again been useful.

One day the Meister came in, pulled out raw potatoes from his pockets and distributed them to the four of us in the pump station. For us this was an amazing event. I asked him quietly where he had gotten the potatoes. He said, "They are from the potato field outside our station. But don't even think of going there — it is outside the perimeter of the construction site, and the guards will shoot you."

But I was very hungry. So, while on night shift, I went to the back of our pump station building and looked around. A railway line lit by lampposts ran just behind the pump station. Two guards with rifles walked in opposite directions along the railway line. I observed that they met close to our building, lit a cigarette, exchanged a few words, and then walked away in opposite directions. I counted how long it took for them to return, calculated the time when the guards would be the farthest away and ran across the railway line into the potato field. I tried to pull the plants out of the ground from the top, but that didn't work, so I dug my hands into the earth under the potatoes and pulled them out that way. I filled my pockets and crawled back toward the railway line, watching out for the guards. After they met and parted again, I waited until the time I had calculated that they would be farthest apart and ran across the line back into the pump station. I had lots of potatoes!

Some of the other guys on my shift saw what I had done and tried the same manoeuvre, only they didn't have the patience to time the guards, as I had. An alarm sounded, and the guards fired some shots into the air; they caught the guys and roughed them up.

When I came back to the barracks with the potatoes I shared them with my father and uncles. We grilled the potatoes by sticking slices on the hot iron stove, then scraping them off and devouring them, skin and all.

The next day, the commandant of our camp instructed the farmer to remove the potatoes that were near the railway line.

~

Every morning we all had to gather on the open field, the *Appellplatz*. We were lined up in rows and counted. If one prisoner was missing, the three thousand or so people in our camp stood outdoors for hours, even on freezing winter days, until the missing prisoner was found. Usually the person was discovered dead in a barracks somewhere. Then the barracks supervisor, a prisoner who was responsible for reporting the dead in his barracks, was beaten. The same counting procedure was repeated on our return from work. The number of prisoners who died at the workplace had to be reported so the numbers could be checked.

One morning, when my pump was ready to restart after a repair, I went to the wall and threw the large switch for the motor to start. There was an explosion and a bright lightning spark lit up in front of my face, totally blinding me. I heard all the pumps run down to a stop. I thought I must have blown the main fuse to the station. The alarm bells went off to alert the other teams to come and clear out all four lines of pipes.

But it was much worse! My broken switch had caused a short-circuit, which had blown out the main transformer in a separate building that fed all three pump buildings. All twelve pipelines had to be cleared at the same time. Several kilometres of pipes! All cement pouring on the huge construction site stopped. I could not see anything, but I heard the construction managers coming. I heard them shouting, "Sabotage!" and I heard talk about hanging me. Then I heard my Meister say in a calm voice, "It is not his fault. The copper bar inside the switch came loose and caused a major short across all three electrical phases."

I sat quietly in the silence of the station. Normally the noise of the four pumps was deafening. At the end of that day, two fellow prisoners took me back to the camp. It took several days for some of my eyesight to return. It took much longer for my sight to fully come back.

I learned later that to replace the blown transformer the Germans had to break a wall in the building housing it. Amazingly, the Germans brought a new transformer by train and within two days had it installed. On the third day after the shutdown, we were pumping again.

I had not intended to sabotage our work, yet for three full days I managed to stop construction of this vital building site! And if not for that Meister, I would likely have been shot or hanged on the spot.

Death by Work

Slowly, we began to settle into the routine of slave labour, working twelve-hour shifts. The day shift was 7:00 a.m. to 7:00 p.m., and the night shift was 7:00 p.m. to 7:00 a.m. Working twelve hours a day is not so bad. I have worked that number of hours often in my life. The problem was that we received far too little nourishment for such work. In the morning, we were given a black liquid, which they called coffee. Once a day we got a bowl of thin soup, without any meat or fat, just some root vegetables and a slice of bread, which kept getting thinner. Every other day, we received a very small portion of cheese, or margarine, or sausage.

Over the next six months we lost our body fat, then our muscles. We became thinner and thinner. Every bone could be seen protruding through our thin skin. We became walking skeletons. Hunger is a very painful experience. Prolonged hunger causes the mind to abandon every thought other than food. When we marched to the workplace and saw an apple core on the road, or a cabbage leaf, ten men would jump to get it. For this the guards would beat us with their rifle butts, hitting us on our backs and forcing us back in line.

At night, I dreamt only of food. My repetitive dream was of my mother's layered Napoleon custard cake, which had always been my birthday cake. Prisoners would often talk about food, reminiscing about meals enjoyed at home before the war, describing in detail every dish, until others would shout, "Stop this talk!"

Every second week we were supposed to have a free Sunday, but for the most part, this did not happen. On a "free" Sunday there would be a demand for, say, forty prisoners to come immediately to unload a train filled with cement. Trains arrived every few hours to the building site, and the fifty-kilogram sacks of cement had to be unloaded into a huge shed.

The guards would grab whoever was around and create a human chain. Two prisoners inside the freight wagon would heave a bag up and drop it on the back of a third prisoner. With the cement on his back, the carrier had to negotiate a narrow plank from the wagon to the shed, and then climb on piles of cement bags laid out in steps to the highest point. Two prisoners stood ready to take the bag off the back of the carrier, who then had to return to the wagon and repeat the run until all the cement was unloaded. After a few hours of this work, we were totally exhausted, barely able to walk back to the camp.

While writing this memoir, I began to question myself as to whether the bags weighed fifty or twenty-five kilos, since in Canada cement bags are twenty-five kilos. I ascertained, through research, that in Germany during the war the bags were indeed fifty. It felt like a ton when that fifty-kilogram bag of cement dropped on my thin sixteen-year-old frame.

To add to the difficulties, the air in the shed was full of cement dust. After working there for half a day, one would cough up cement and sneeze cement for days. I felt sorry for the prisoners who had to work in that shed day after day, cutting open the sacks and pouring the cement powder into a screw pump that pumped the dry cement to our pump stations.

If you slowed down during this work, you were the recipient of a vicious kick or beating. One of our camp commandants specialized in kicking prisoners at the back of the leg, a few inches above the heel. When a prisoner collapsed from the pain, he was subjected to more kicking until he got up and joined the line. Everything in the concentration camps had to be done at a running gait — it was part of the intimidation system.

~

When my shoes from the ghetto finally wore out and fell apart, I removed the gold coin hidden in the heel before abandoning them. Then I had to use the wooden clogs issued to us, which caused wounds on my feet. My father found a man who would take the coin in exchange for a pair of better clogs — which had a leather top — and two loaves of bread. The bread was to be delivered in quarter portions over several days, but we only received three portions before the buyer disappeared. At least the new shoes, though they still wounded my feet, allowed me to continue working.

As winter approached, I worried about my father. He was working outside on the construction site, carrying fifty-kilogram bags of cement. I asked the Meister to permit my father to work in our station. The Meister said that he could not work with us, but he could work in the hut next to our station where the corks for cleaning the concrete pipes were being made. My father's new job was to soak empty cement bags in water, then fold and roll them to the correct diameter and tie them with wire, making a cork. It was a good place to work, as there were no construction supervisors to target him and it was warm indoors. If he prepared a good stack of corks, there was no pressure. One thing, however, soon became clear: the water and cement began to attack the skin on my father's hands, making it raw and painful. I gave him grease from the workshop to protect his hands, and that helped a bit.

Working in the pumping station saved both my life and my father's. If we had been assigned to work on the actual construction, outdoors, in winter, dressed in our flimsy clothes, we would surely have perished. Many prisoners died working on the dangerous construction site. They had to stand on a narrow, wet and slippery board in the middle of a forest of steel rods sprouting all around and control the heavy vertical pipe hanging from a crane, which was feeding the mixed concrete into the space below. The wind sometimes swung the pipe sideways and pushed the prisoner off the board. He would fall into the concrete and drown, his body encased in the hardening concrete.

One day, one of my friends did not return to the barracks after work. "Where is Shmuel?" I asked. "In the concrete," came the answer. Many years later, I found out that twelve prisoners had been buried in the concrete.

Many prisoners died from the back-breaking work. Those who were older or had bad hearts or diabetes and received no medication died first. But then the young, healthy men began to die, too. Much later, I read somewhere that the Germans called this "Tod durch Arbeit," death by work. That was obviously the plan, for new prisoners could always be brought in.

One morning, I woke up when the whistle blew and saw that my friend who slept next to me was not moving. I tried to shake him. He was dead. The first thing I did was check his pockets to see if there was a piece of bread there (we used to try to keep some bread for the morning, when the hunger was the hardest to bear), but it seemed he had eaten his the night before. I carried out his body — he did not weigh much — with the help of another prisoner. I carried more dead bodies in this camp than I could count.

As if hunger and unbearable work conditions were not enough of a punishment, we became infested with lice. There was a total absence of washing facilities in the camp. In summer, we at least had water taps outside; in winter, they were frozen. Thousands of these six-legged bugs were on each one of us, hiding in the seams of our clothing and drinking our blood. We scratched incessantly. These lice also brought spotted typhus fever, a microbial disease transmitted through their feces.

I became ill with this typhus, had a very high fever and lost consciousness for several days. Many people died while unconscious with the high fever caused by this illness. I woke up in the hospital barracks after several days. My father came to see me, and he later told me that I had whispered to him, "I am so hungry! I want an apple." Where do you find an apple in Dachau?! I must have been delirious to say that. But in the evening, my father went to the window that was at the back of the camp kitchen, when even going close to the kitchen was a dangerous thing for him to do. Luckily, there was a woman working there who knew me — she was an older student who attended my school before the war. My father told her what I had said, and she gave him three little green apples. He brought me the three apples, refusing to take even one for himself. I ate all three. They were the tastiest apples I have ever eaten.

After I recovered from my bout of spotted typhus, I was still very weak, and Dr. Benjamin Zacharin, who had been in the Kovno ghetto, offered me the chance to work in the *Krankenstube*, the hospital barracks, where he was in charge — a life-saving gesture. There, I cleaned, helped the sick and did anything else that needed doing.

Dr. Zacharin had been a surgeon in the Jewish hospital before the war and was the head of the health department of the ghetto hospital. My mother had worked for him as a surgical nurse, my uncle Gedalie had been the administrator of the ghetto hospital and my father also worked there for a time. He knew our whole family well.

I believe that sometimes Dr. Zacharin had the responsibility of deciding when to send a sick prisoner, who was not likely to work again, to another Kaufering subcamp that some referred to as the Schonung Lager, the so-called Protection Camp; but the Kaufering IV subcamp was a place where people mostly died of hunger. Once, he told me that he thought my father should be sent there, due to his badly swollen legs. I told him that if my father was sent away, I would go with him. Dr. Zacharin thought about it and relented. After the war, my mother told me that she and Zacharin had promised each other that she would look after his wife if they ended up in the same camp, and that he, in turn, would look after me and my father. I was aware that my mother and Zacharin had a romantic, yet platonic, relationship in the ghetto.

After Dachau was liberated, Dr. Zacharin returned to Lithuania, contrary to the advice of my uncle Gedalie. He felt that he could function well in the Russian language, under communism, and he thought that he would regain his previous position as surgeon, which he did, initially. Then other prisoners from Dachau returned to Kaunas, and accusations were raised that Zacharin had sent some of them to the Schonung Lager. He was jailed by the Soviets for being a collaborator, and he died in prison — a very sad ending after surviving Dachau. I remember him fondly.

~

One day, we observed a car with a huge red cross on its side parked outside the camp gates. Two men in suits were standing nearby and talking to the commandant. Later, we were given a small card with the symbol of the Red Cross on it and we were told to write our full names on the card and sign it. The text stated that we confirmed having received a food parcel from the Red Cross. Some of us were of the opinion that we should not sign the card until we received the parcel, while others said that we might get a beating for refusing to sign. We all signed.

The next day we received a small carton that had been opened and was partially empty. Inside were a half-kilogram of sugar, a small tin of condensed milk, a tin of sardines and one packet of cigarettes. It was obvious that the carton had originally contained more stuff. Nonetheless, we ate the sardines with delight, and I exchanged my cigarettes for more sardines. We licked the sugar and could not stop, putting some of it in the coffee in the morning, which made us delirious with pleasure.

Dr. Zacharin advised me to put some of the sugar I received from the Red Cross on a wound I had showed him on my right leg, close to the ankle, and not to bandage it. I had been having a problem with this wound for months. I'd gone to the hospital barracks before I even started working there and asked if I could put Vaseline on it and have it bandaged, but nothing helped. The wound would not heal; it had been getting larger and was now three inches long.

The sugar soaked up the ooze and hardened over the wound. I added more sugar whenever I saw moisture coming to the surface. About three weeks later, the hardened coating over the wound peeled off, and clean new skin was revealed. Cured by sugar! I thanked Dr. Zacharin, and he told me that long ago, when he had studied medicine in Russia, he had been taught a folk medicine class on curing wounds using honey, so he thought perhaps sugar would have the same effect. Sugar is an antiseptic — no microbes can survive in sugar, apparently. I still have a mark on my leg in that spot.

We were all disgusted with the Red Cross for not coming into the camp to observe our living conditions and our state of hunger. We were also very upset that they allowed themselves to be hoodwinked by the Nazis, allowing them to steal whatever else had been in the parcels, probably chocolate.

My unhappiness with the Red Cross Society never subsided — I have never contributed one cent to them. I know that they do good work in the world, and it is silly to carry a grudge for so long, especially since the Red Cross admitted, after the war, that they let down the concentration camp prisoners. Still, I know that the Red Cross did an excellent job for the Allied prisoners of war, transmitting parcels and mail from home and making sure they were received, but for the Jews in the camps....

~

After the terrible, hard winter of 1944–1945, our prisoner population had been reduced considerably. Many simply died of hunger, some of wounds that would not heal. Some were so exhausted, their feet swollen from malnutrition, that they could no longer work. They were selected by a visiting SS doctor and were shipped off, either to Auschwitz — up until November 1944 — or to the Schonung Lager, where they were left to die, with minimal food rations even compared to our rations in the working camp. My half-uncle, Zalman Knebel, died there. His son, my cousin Chone Knebel, survived in our camp.

It was dangerous to be admitted to the hospital barracks, the *Krankenstube*, since a selection could come at any time. One day my father came to the hospital, exhausted, his legs swollen from hunger again. This time, Dr. Zacharin admitted him. The very next day, an SS doctor came to inspect the patients. All the patients had to go outside and stand in line, naked, to be reviewed by the SS doctor. A truck was idling nearby, ready to receive the patients selected for removal. As staff, I was standing outside watching how the doctor selected people with swollen legs to go to the truck. I ran around the corner to see where my father was. He was standing in line to be examined. I went into the latrine nearby and motioned to him to come to me. He did not want to lose his place in the queue, so he waved to me to wait till after he passed the selection. I waved more urgently, and I could tell he was irritated, but a prisoner behind him said, "Your son is calling you, go see what he wants." So, he came to me, cross that I had made him leave the line. I pulled him into the latrine and explained that people like him, with swollen legs, were being taken away. I kept him in the latrine until the selection was over and the doctor and the truck left. I saved his life yet again.

The Three Commandants

Camp commandants were in complete charge of our camp and our lives, and terrifying in their total power. Any one of them could turn into the Angel of Death at any moment. They gave orders without hesitation, without the possibility of an appeal. They were judge, jury and executioner.

I never discovered anything about the men behind the SS masks. We never got to hear their names; "Der Kommandant" was all we needed to know. Even their rank — SS *Obersturmführer*, which is equivalent to lieutenant — was seldom heard in the camp because other SS officers and soldiers did not, as a rule, address them by their rank. Commandants came and went, each with his own idiosyncrasies. They were allegedly brought in for a while to recuperate at a cushy job in the camp after serving on the front lines. Then they were shipped off to the front again to fight the Allies. We believed that they left unwillingly, particularly when sent to the Soviet front.

Of those I remember, one was a musician, one appeared to be a medical student and another was a vicious, crude guy with a potty mouth. There were others who I barely remember. Among ourselves we assigned them nicknames, and that is how I remember them.

The Musician
I cannot remember whether he was short or tall, but I recall the unusual sight of him walking around the camp with a violin in his

hands. Sometimes he played a simple tune, some *Volkslied*, folk song. We thought that he must have been a village musician before the war. He had a finely chiseled face and often looked sad. He did his job without the enthusiasm of a real believer in the task. Naturally, he did not last long in our camp. But before he was sent back to the front lines he undertook one interesting project.

As usual, before going to work, we stood for roll call on the *Appellplatz*. We were already used to the lengthy procedure of counting the living and laying out the prisoners who had died during the night. When the total showed that not one soul, living or dead, was missing, we could march away to work. But one morning the commandant had an unusual request: "If there are any musicians among you, step forward now."

There sure were! A sizable number of musicians, including the conductor Misha (Michael) Hofmekler and a famous violinist, Alexander Stupel, had lived in Kaunas when the Soviets occupied Lithuania in 1940. When the German army came in 1941 they were confined in the ghetto with the other Jews from Kaunas, and Hofmekler conducted the ghetto's orchestra. There were many other fine musicians amongst the Kaunas Jews.

People hesitated — it is never good to be singled out in a concentration camp; we couldn't tell what awaited us. The unwritten rule for survival in the camp was: Try to be invisible. March in the middle of a row, not at the edge. Never march in the first row, or in the last. Be lost in the crowd.

The commandant waited in silence until several people stepped forward, haltingly. He told the rest of us to fill up the lines. There always had to be five people in a line. We were marched out to the worksite, leaving the apprehensive musicians in camp. We debated in whispers what "The Musician" wanted with them.

We had to wait until the end of our twelve-hour shift, march back to the camp, stand for the second roll call, line up for the soup, the one slice of bread, and perhaps a square inch by a quarter inch of cheese or margarine, then walk into the barracks, before we learned what happened to the musicians.

The Musician had asked each prisoner for his history and what instruments he played. He told them, "You are not to go to work. I am going to create an orchestra, and you will need to practice for a concert." The musicians became bolder when they heard this and respectfully informed him that they were so hungry that playing properly would be difficult. This was in the late summer of 1944, when we had already been in this camp about a month, and we were starving. "No problem," The Musician announced grandly. "I will tell the kitchen to give you as much soup and bread as you can eat!" Well, this was really good news for the musicians!

A few days later a pile of instruments arrived. A barracks was cleared out for the musicians, and music stands and chairs were brought in (we had never seen a chair in the camp). The commandant began to visit the barracks every morning after the roll call, when the camp was quiet because the night shift was sleeping and the day shift was at work. He discussed what music should be prepared for the concert he was planning. I was not there, but I heard that he listened to advice and had some suggestions of his own. He also asked the musicians to suggest some Jewish music, and the musicians, after discussion, thought of *Kol Nidrei* by Max Bruch. Max Bruch (1838–1920), a German composer, was a Protestant who had created this piece after a Jewish cantor introduced him to the plaintive melody of the Yom Kippur (Day of Atonement) prayer of the same name. The tune is very familiar to any Jew who attends prayers. They also selected something by Mozart, and several lighter pieces from Viennese operettas.

The musicians started to eat, put some flesh on their bones and began to look like they belonged to a race different from the rest of us. At the end of the summer, the commandant announced that we were going to have a concert in the camp on a Sunday, and that visitors would be present. Sunday was not a resting day for everyone; we worked for two weeks nonstop and then were supposed to have one Sunday off, which, as I mentioned, sometimes did not happen. The work at the construction site could not stop, so we rotated in groups, getting the Sunday off at various times. There were always some prisoners around the camp on Sunday afternoons after a day shift the previous day, and I was among them.

The day before the concert, wooden boards were brought in and laid out to cover the mud in the open square in the centre of the camp, where the daily roll call took place. Around the periphery, on three sides, were placed benches for the visiting audience. The following day, Sunday, in the early afternoon, all prisoners who were in camp were told to gather in rows of five and to line up in columns on one side of the concert area. The commandant was very excited. He was running around in a sweat, dealing with all the details like a mother at a wedding.

In the early afternoon, the camp gates were opened, and the visitors began arriving — officers in uniform, with their wives or girlfriends; townspeople in dark suits and ties, the women in summer dresses, white gloves and large summer hats. What a strange sight these guests were to us! A touch of remembrance of normal life in this miserable camp. A modestly hot sun was shining indiscriminately on the whole Bavarian landscape and on our camp.

The guests sat down on the benches. The musicians were already sitting on the platform. The commandant loudly instructed us, the prisoners standing at attention, to be "At ease." He gave a little speech to the guests, welcoming them to the Prisoner Orchestra Concert, loudly announced the name of the first piece — *Kol Nidrei* — and waved to the conductor to proceed.

We prisoners did not expect to hear the plaintive tune of the song that starts the Yom Kippur service during the holiest day of the year for Jews! We were astounded, and then struck with grief. Our tears flowed freely. The greatest novelist could not make up a scene like this. At the end of each musical number, the guests seemed uncertain whether it was okay to applaud. There was some hesitant, gentle clapping. Then the concert was over, and the guests filed out, throwing us prisoners sidelong glances.

The following week, a new commandant appeared in the camp for morning roll call. The Musician was gone, probably sent to the Soviet front.

I heard that this new commandant walked around the camp after the morning shift had departed for work and heard music playing. He followed his ears and came upon the barracks occupied by the musicians. He opened the door and looked in. The musicians immediately stopped practicing, jumped up and removed their caps — standard behaviour when any officer or guard entered. The commandant looked around and asked, "What are you doing?" "Practicing, sir," came the reply. "Practicing for what?" asked the commandant. One musician answered, "We don't know, sir. The previous commandant told us to practice every day, so we practice." "Out of here, you lazy Jewish swine!" the commandant shrieked, and stepped away from the door.

The musicians ran outside, each one receiving a kick in the ass from the agile commandant on the way out. Then the commandant grabbed some instruments and smashed them on the floor. Finally, he turned to the terrified members of the orchestra and shouted, "Tomorrow you go back to work with everyone else! Lazy swine!"

Obviously this commandant did not like music.

The Medical Student

I don't really know whether he was a medical student, but his interest in medicine became clear very soon after he arrived.

The new commandant came into the hospital barracks to be shown around by our doctor. He asked where the operating theatre was. Dr. Zacharin told him that we did not have one and said, "Anyway, the prisoners are so undernourished that there would be no point operating on them." The commandant was not satisfied with the answer and insisted we needed an operating room. Dr. Zacharin told him that we had no equipment. "Give me a list of requirements," said the commandant. The doctor prepared an extensive list of the equipment required. He hoped to get rid of him that way.

Two weeks later two huge crates arrived. I was told to unpack them. Inside was everything the doctor had put on his list and, in fact, much more! Even a whole pack of vitamins by Hoffmann-La Roche of Switzerland. I made use of all the vitamins we received in the shipment, getting permission from the doctor to distribute the vitamin C and E to the patients. They loved it — something to put in their mouths — and they begged for more.

Dr. Zacharin instructed me to build an operating room. I constructed an operating table made of wood, padded with blankets. I laid out all the equipment and connected the sterilizers.

Every day the commandant came in and asked whether there were any operations planned for the day. One day a patient came in and was diagnosed with an appendix attack. Dr. Zacharin said, "We might as well operate; he will die anyway." The commandant was informed about the impending operation, and Dr. Zacharin told me that I would be assisting. I pleaded total ignorance in these matters, telling him that I was a metal worker. I suggested that he ask the other doctor who worked in the hospital barracks, but he refused, saying, "That doctor was an internist and knows nothing of surgery. Your mother knew how to do it, and you will too." Apparently, he thought that skills got transmitted through generations by DNA....

I asked what I should do, and he showed me how to sterilize the instruments and prepare all the swabs and bandages. He told me to boil two pairs of operating gloves since we did not have a special sterilizer for that purpose. I put the gloves in a pot of water and boiled them just before the operation. The doctor came in and asked for the gloves, so I pulled them out with a tweezers from the pot. He looked at the gloves, full of water and asked, "How can I put them on if they are wet inside?" "I was also wondering about that," I said. He gave a grunt and said that I should have tied them up first. I thought back to the blacksmith in the ghetto.

The commandant was there, standing at a respectful distance with his hands behind his back. Our doctor injected the patient, putting him under, and the operation began. Dr. Zacharin was also a professor of surgery before the war; now he had an audience, so he began a commentary about what he was doing. When he asked me to hand him instruments, he pointed carefully at them so that I would know which ones he meant. He cut open the patient, pulled out the appendix, which was green and brown with infection, tied it up and removed it. He then closed up the patient, sewing the stitches with remarkable dexterity. A happy ending — this prisoner survived the war!

We had a second operation — a patient had a twisted bowel and an operation was unavoidable. The Medical Student had another lecture in surgery. That prisoner would have survived too, but he later died of hunger.

Soon after that second operation the Medical Student was replaced by a new commandant, who never set foot in the hospital.

The Last Commandant

He had one name only for us prisoners: "Assholes." It sounds even worse in German! We reciprocated and called him by precisely the same name. His real name was Otto Förschner.

By this time we knew that Germany had lost the war and that the American army was very close. This last commandant knew it too and felt sore that the Germans lost the war, and he was vicious. He appeared to always be in a bad mood and would hit us and kick us for the slightest reason. In the mornings during *Appell*, when the Allied bombers flew overhead, he would make us lie face down in the mud. If he saw someone lift his head to look at the planes, he would kick him and force his head down into the mud with his boot.

One morning, when spring was in the air and he noticed that we looked a little hopeful, he gave us a talk: "You assholes, you think that you will survive the war and be free? Let me assure you that we are keeping the last bullet for you. No matter how the war ends, you will not survive. So forget about it." We had good reason to believe him.

~

I have read the proceedings of the first Dachau war crimes trial in November 1945, which took place about seven months after the liberation of Dachau by the American army. The trial was managed by the American army when the first forty accused men who served in Dachau and the outside camps, like Kaufering I — my camp — were tried.

Förschner was condemned to death and was hanged at Landsberg prison on May 28, 1946. Most of the others accused in that trial were also executed. They are all buried in a church cemetery within sight of the Landsberg prison, where Hitler had been locked up in 1924. I visited the site in 2010, while attending commemoration events at Dachau sixty-five years after liberation. All the graves are unmarked, but they have a cross on them. My well-informed guide and friend, Lieutenant Colonel Gerhard Roletscheck of the German air force, showed me which grave was Förschner's. I did not dance on his grave, but my mind did....

My Moment of Liberation

April 24, 1945. Konzentrationslager Dachau, Lager I, near Kaufering. The war was coming to an end. The Allies were flying over our area with no resistance from the German air force. The work on our construction site stopped.

We were told that our camp was being closed and all able prisoners would be marched out to a new destination. My father was still in the hospital barracks with swollen legs, and in his weakened state he would not have survived one day of the march. I told him to stay with me and the other sick prisoners in the hospital. There was the risk that tying our fate to the sick prisoners would lead to certain death, but for my father there was no choice, and I decided to stay with him. After the marchers left the camp it was announced that all hospital inmates would go by train.

My father and I, together with the sick prisoners, were led out of the camp. After walking in a heavy rain for two hours, we saw a freight train waiting for us. We were a mass of emaciated men, standing in almost total darkness, awaiting our unknown fate. With difficulty, we climbed into the freight wagons. I urged my father to lie down flat, not to sit, but I would not give him my reason for this instruction. I hadn't told him of the task I had been given the previous day.

Of all the misery I had witnessed in the past nine months in Kaufering, that last day was the most horrifying. A group of us had been taken outside the camp to unload a train. But this time it was not bags of cement to unload — it was dead and dying prisoners. A train full of prisoners from a nearby camp had been shot at by an Allied fighter plane. The guards had run into the nearby forest during the attack, but the railcars, with the prisoners inside, had been locked.

When we arrived at the train, and the guards opened the doors, a shocking sight greeted us. The prisoners inside were horribly wounded, with blood all over them, or they were already dead. We saw arms and legs covered in blood and lying at unnatural angles. It was our task to lift these people out of the rail cars and lay them on the grass. The living were crying and begging for water. We had no water to give them. We piled the lucky dead on the side and left the wounded prisoners on the grass to bleed to death — abandoned, in agony and alone.

I was totally shaken by this experience. Carrying dead people was one thing, but these prisoners, crying with pain…I was totally shaken. I did not tell my father what I had seen, since I did not want to upset him too. Now we were in a locked freight car, and I could imagine quite vividly another attack from the air. I had seen the large bullet holes a few inches apart that had torn through the lower third of the rail cars, and I knew what damage those bullets could do. I wanted my father to lie flat to avoid the bullets. When I mentioned the possibility of an air attack, he began to talk to me soothingly, like I was losing touch with reality.

We travelled undisturbed, and our train arrived at the large marshalling yard at the main camp of Dachau. We were now at the first concentration camp established under Hitler in Germany in 1933. The doors opened with a screech and the SS armed guards were screaming "Raus!" (Get out!) We were stiff from sitting in wet clothes in the cold wagon and could hardly stretch our legs, but to avoid a whack on the back with a rifle butt, we fell from the high rail cars to the ground and ran in the direction indicated. The rail yard stank with that distinctive smell of rotting bodies — many trains had arrived from different concentration camps, and some had been attacked by the Allied fighter planes. The dead and dying prisoners had not been removed from the trains for several days, we were told later.

Our first stop in the main camp was a shower house. We had our first shower in nine months! Lukewarm water and some carbolic smelling liquid soap helped us wash off the dirt and the lice that had tormented us. The Germans were afraid of an outbreak of epidemics in the camp. All our clothes were taken from us, and we were issued another set of striped jackets and pants, with no regard to the size. Then we were driven at a trot into one of the barracks.

Thirty-two large barracks had initially been designed to hold six thousand prisoners in total; now, each barracks held close to a thousand prisoners in each. When we arrived at our designated barracks, the four levels of wooden bunks were already greatly overloaded. My father grabbed a spot on the lowest bunk when a dead body was removed. He lay down there, amid the weak and the dying. I lay down on the floor near him.

In the morning, prisoners brought in a large drum full of hot tea. We lined up to receive our portion. My only possessions were an aluminium bowl and a spoon. If I lost them, I would likely die. I kept the bowl strapped to my clothing, the spoon hanging on a string tied to a buttonhole.

I knew my father was going to die very soon. I recognized all the signs: swollen legs; glazed, unfocused, grey eyes; a shuffling gait; a very soft voice. My father was ready to die; he had already given up. For so long we had clung to each other, helped each other, and now I was losing my father. I knew that soon either the Germans would kill us all, like the last commandant had promised us, or the American army would arrive and free us, but my father would not make it. I feared I would find him dead in the morning, and I thought of my mother, whose fate was unknown to me. A deep sadness overcame me. I remember thinking, *Please, don't go.* But my father was still with me the next morning, talking weakly to me.

April 29, 1945. That morning, my father did not get up at all. At noon, when the daily food ration arrived, I urged him to come and line up for the soup and bread, but he could not get up. He asked me to take his bowl and collect his ration for him. I stood in line and explained that the second bowl was for my father lying in the bunk. The orderly poured another portion of soup and gave me another slice of bread — our whole daily ration. I walked back to my father and he eagerly took the bowl of soup from me.

Suddenly there arose a great noise in the barracks — people were shouting, "The Americans are here! We are free!" Through the window I saw a Jeep with a five-pointed star. I said, "Father, we are free, the Americans have arrived." He looked at me with some incomprehension on his face and said, "That's good. Do you have the bread?"

This was my moment of liberation — "Do you have the bread?"

I still feared that my father would die, even though we were liberated. But an hour later he climbed out from the bunk, stood in front of me and asked, "So now what?"

He was fifty-four and he had survived! I saw a change in him and knew that now he would live. I believe that hope gave him strength when he most needed it. Liberation, for me, was tied to my father living. But life after liberation really did feel like, So now what? After about four and a half years, the war was finally over for us. I had just turned seventeen, I weighed seventy pounds, and I owned a soup bowl and a spoon.

Both survivors and American liberators have described the aftermath of the liberation of Dachau as horrific. The Americans were appalled by what they saw. They emptied their own supplies and gave us what they had. Then they opened the storehouses and began distributing whatever food they found there. They gave me and my father a two-pound tin of processed bully beef. I didn't have tools to open the tin, but I was able to hack an opening with the edge of a knife. My father and I collected little pieces of paper, and we managed to make a fire. In our little metal can we boiled the meat with some water. We watched each other to ensure we were not eating too much; we just drank the soup. We hadn't had any real food for close to a year, and we knew we couldn't digest the meat. All the survivors were so hungry, and many couldn't control themselves around this new food — they ate too much and died. We saw the Americans taking out huge wagons filled with dead bodies.

American guards were at the gates and didn't let us out. Slowly, they emptied the overcrowded barracks. Within a few days my father and I were taken outside the main camp to a barracks that the guards must have used, as they were clean and had only two levels of bunks. Some doctors came to examine us.

Then the questions arose. What were we going to do? Where were we going to go? We decided that we would not go to Lithuania or to the Soviet Union. Suddenly, this became an issue. The Soviets were the first to come and offer to take their citizens back to their homeland by airplane. They went door to door calling out names of all the Russian Republics. We did not answer their call, which was a good decision. The first few were taken by plane, then the rest by train. We later learned that as soon as they crossed into Soviet territory, they were accused of being traitors and collaborators with the Nazis and they again became prisoners and were treated abominably.

We stayed in the barracks in Dachau for several more weeks. At first, we stayed in bed, sleeping for long hours. Then we started to feel a little better, but we were far from well. It felt like our lives were in limbo.

$\sim$

In May 1945, my paternal uncle, Samuel Gotz, who lived in Southern Rhodesia, Africa, received a telegram from Hertze Missulawin of Johannesburg, a relative of the Gotz family. It was the first notice to our relatives that we survived the war.

[Telegram sent from Samuel Gotz to Hertze Missulawin, 1945.[6]]

I try to imagine the moment when my uncle Samuel received this telegram from Hertze Missulawin saying that his brother Judel had survived Dachau. The last letters from us in Kaunas, Lithuania, must have reached Samuel around June 1941 at the latest. After July 1941, no letters from us left Lithuania — Germany had already occupied our country and there was war.

～

After about a week, my uncles Tanchum and Gedalie, who survived a death march and were liberated outside Dachau, turned up looking

---

6   *The Zionist Record* was a Jewish newspaper in Johannesburg, South Africa, that published lists of people who were reported as survivors of the concentration camps in Europe.

for us. They said we had to get out of the camp and go to a hospital. My other uncle, David, was with us. They organized the transportation, and a truck drove us all to St. Ottilien, near the village of Geltendorf, in Bavaria. St. Ottilien was a monastery that, during the war, ran a military hospital. The American administration had discharged the German patients, and the hospital took us in, together with a lot of other Jewish displaced persons who had been liberated in the area.

The St. Ottilien hospital was staffed by nuns. Three Jewish doctors, survivors, were already working there, together with some German doctors and nurses. It was a proper hospital that began to deal with all our ailments. We were given lots of vitamins. One nun would come in every day and sing, "Vitaminen, Vitaminen." We called her the "Vitaminen Nun." The nuns were very kind. At first, they were afraid of us, only doing their duties. Later, when they realized that we didn't regard them as the enemy, they softened up. They tried to keep some order.

My father was still very weak. To help him smoke his cigarettes, I would go over to a patient who had a lighter and light up for him. A puff here and a puff there, and I began to smoke too. I thought I might have tuberculosis (TB), since I had a lung infection when I was a child, and I asked for X-rays. The doctors told me there was a calcified area in my lungs, but no TB. Anyway, I made myself give up smoking.

At liberation, as I mentioned, I weighed seventy pounds. Now I was gaining five pounds a week, I was eating and not moving much. I began to fatten up, and I developed a big stomach. I still felt so weak that going up even one flight of stairs required a huge effort. I spent my time in a large room with dozens of beds, just sleeping and chatting with the men and boys in the room. A huge crucifix with a very pained-looking Christ hung at the end of the room. We slept in its shadow.

All discussions revolved around a few subjects: how we all hated the Germans and the other nations amongst whom we lived for thousands of years and who often betrayed us in our hour of need; how the American Jews would surely try to help us to get out of Germany and start new lives; our families, whose fates were unknown or, worse, known already; how to find cigarettes; and listing to each other the many miracles that had pulled us from death's door. People were discussing what they were going to do after they got out of the hospital and were sure that after what we had endured, the world would look after us, that we would be invited to come to America, France or other countries. Of course, this turned out to be pure imagination. Then there was talk of revenge. We were so weak that getting out of bed was an effort, but many people were nonetheless dreaming of revenge.

Some of the hospital's wings were full of women, all survivors. Slowly we began to meet with them, always searching for information about loved ones. "Where are you from and which camp were you in?" was always the first question, to find out if they knew anyone from your town, perhaps someone from your family.

Ten days after liberation my father found a small piece of paper somewhere, asked for a pencil and wrote his first letter to his brother and his uncle in Africa.

May 9, 1945
Dear brother Samuel and wife,[7] dear Uncle Isaac!

We can report to you that we, that is my son, Elinka [diminutive for Elly], *my brothers-in-law Gedalie, David and Tanchum and I are alive, and we are together here. We belong to the 10 per cent of Jews that remained alive from Hitler's slaughters. But sadly, sadly, my dears, we still do not know where our dear beloved Sonja is now, and whether she is*

---

7 Julius did not remember the name of Samuel's wife, Ann, as Samuel married her in Africa and Julius had never met her.

still alive. After being deported from Kovno, the women were separated from the men at a certain station, and we are still unable to find out where they are. Elinka and I have both had spotted typhus and difficult illnesses, and I have joint rheumatism as well and therefore find it difficult to write. Generally, we are, Elinka and I, still very weak after all these terrible travails. We need help. We do not know, however, where we will end up staying. Today we are leaving Dachau and are travelling somewhere. At the first opportunity, I will let you know where we will be.

How are you? How is your wife? How are you doing in business?

Elly had studied locksmithing in the ghetto, and despite his youthful age — he was just fifteen and a half years old — had shown so much capability that he became an instructor in the trade school for locksmithing and was teaching forty-five children the trade.

We were asked where in the world we have friends and where we would like to go. Elinka and I said Africa or Palestine, but it is very possible that we will have to go back to Russia. Now the most important thing for us is to find Sonja. Wherever we end up in Germany with Elinka and the brothers-in-law, we will place ourselves in a hospital; we should get stronger, and then we will question what's next.

We have things to tell that will last generations — Egypt[8] was child's play compared with what we went through.

...

Keep well my dear ones,
Your Judel

---

8 Referring to the biblical story of the Jews being slaves in Egypt.

Free of Hate

After many weeks, I forced myself to go out and walk around the gardens. I found a gymnastics bar mounted between two metal posts, and I started to exercise. At first, I couldn't even hold on to the bar. Twice a day I would go down to the garden area and try to hang on the bar and lift my legs. Gradually, my muscles responded, and eventually I could swing myself over the bar.

As I explored the wider area around the monastery, I came across a large, fully equipped workshop with lathes and machines, where the monks did the repairs of all the farm machinery and everything else required for the monastery. There was no chitchat; they worked in silence.

I approached a monk and told him I wanted to work. He said, "We don't pay. We ourselves don't get paid." I explained that I did not expect to be paid, I just wanted to work again. Reluctantly, he accepted me. I would go in after breakfast and ask if there was something to do. At first, he gave me very simple tasks, mostly on crude farm machinery, but he later gave me more complicated jobs. I told him I knew about locks, and he gave me work to do with locks. Once I did a difficult repair on a large, ancient lock and he was pleased with me. I enjoyed the work, which gave my life some focus.

I soon became aware that my head was full of thoughts about exacting revenge on the Germans. Every German man of a certain age was a suspect in my mind, and I daydreamed about what I would do: Poison them in large numbers? Lay some explosives somewhere? When I visited Munich, I saw the immense destruction caused by Allied bombing, and I realized that the Germans had also suffered in the war, but I did not think that was enough. I was full of hate, of anger. So many scenes of the Germans' brutality during the war years were spinning around in my memory.

One day it occurred to me that my thoughts were busy with the wrong issues. Instead of thinking about my own future, what I wanted from life, I was daydreaming about revenge, letting my anger play with ideas that were surely not realistic. I decided that I was not a killer and was not going to become one.

When I freed myself from these feelings of hate, I felt that I started living again. I asked myself, what am I going to do with my life? I remembered my dream from before the war to become an engineer. Every time my thoughts returned to revenge, I turned them around and dreamt of my future. It took a while, but eventually I came to accept that I could not hate a whole people — hating that way was what Hitler had taught! That man walking on the street could have been a vicious camp commandant or a professor of history who hated the Nazis. The woman on the train was likely brought up in the Nazi movement as a girl but never did any harm to anyone. I forced myself to give up the hate, and I did succeed after a while. I practiced stopping certain thoughts immediately after they started and changing the subject by refocusing on good thoughts.

Many years later, in Canada, my daughter Julia told me a saying: "To hate is like taking poison and hoping the other will die." Many people attribute this quote to Buddha, though it is also attributed to a variety of sources. Regardless, I feel like I tasted that poison at age seventeen, but I spit it out, and never tasted it again. Now, whenever I am speaking to students, I quote this saying.

At around this time the United Nations Relief and Rehabilitation Administration (UNRRA) was displaying lists with the names of people who were liberated from concentration camps in Germany.

The lists were typewritten, and with multiple carbon copies, the type had become so pale that one could hardly read them. When someone discovered a member of their family on the list there was great excitement and they were congratulated. There was always the hope that the next day you would find someone from your own family on the list. It was a very emotional time. There was always the question, "Am I totally alone, or is there someone from my family left?"

Every day we left our hospital room and went downstairs to read the latest lists, and every day we went back to our rooms with our heads bent in sadness. I needed my mother to come back. I slept, I ate and I took the vitamins they were giving us every day, but I was listless and showed little interest in anything.

Then the day came when life began to look different to me — my mother was alive! On July 20, 1945, we saw the names of my mother and my aunt Mary on the list. They were in a hospital in Kiel, a city in northern Germany. We had found them! Our excitement cannot be described. I could not stop envisioning what it would be like to see my mother again.

At the end of August, my uncles Tanchum and Gedalie received Permission to Travel documents, which allowed them to travel by train and truck. Travel was difficult because trains were not running on schedule. It took more than a month for my two uncles to manage to travel to Kiel — in unpredictable trains with broken windows — and to come back, bringing my mother and my aunt Mary to St. Ottilien. At the same time, my uncle Tanchum met Nata, who was friends with my mother and aunt in the hospital, and he brought her back with them. Later, they got married.

Finally, my mother was back with me! I was totally overcome with a deep happiness that I did not know how to express. She hugged me for a very long time, kept looking at me, asked me a thousand questions and hugged me again. She had already heard about our time in the camps from my uncles, but she wanted to hear the stories again from me and my father. We all sat for hours listening to one another's experiences, to stories of all the small turns that life took in the camps, turns that meant life or death, that happened to be the right ones each time. We all felt that a string of miracles had allowed us to survive and meet again. My father often wiped a tear as we sat there, listening and telling.

Here is the letter my father wrote his brother on the day we saw my mother's and my aunt's names on the list.

July 20, 1945

My Dear Ones!

I am quickly letting you know that our dear Sonja has been found. She is in Kiel, in North Germany. We expect her here in ten to twelve days. It turns out that she survived through a great miracle, like all of us. The Germans, prior to losing the war, loaded four hundred women under a yellow flag (to indicate pestilence) and no one would let them near. The American (or the English) aircraft bombarded the ship, and it caught fire close to shore and started sinking. The desperate women were standing on deck, blackened by the smoke, and calling for help.... Sixty women were saved. The others were burnt or drowned.[9]

Amongst the saved ones were Sonja and my sister-in-law [David's wife, Mary], *whose hand was shot through. This all happened two and a half months ago.*

---

9 Elly's father is reporting what he heard at the time. Current research indicates that on May 3, 1945, at least four German ships — *Cap Arcona, Thielbek, Deutschland* and *Athen* — were anchored in the Bay of Lübeck on the Baltic Sea; some of these ships were holding approximately 9,000 concentration camp prisoners. Reports about the Nazis' plans for the prisoners varies — some sources state the SS planned to sink the ships; other sources state that the ships were en route to Norway or Sweden. But the British Royal Air Force (RAF), having received information that these were military ships packed with Nazi officers, bombed the *Cap Arcona, Deutschland* and the *Thielbek*. At least 7,000 people died in this tragedy — from the *Cap Arcona* there were 350 survivors, and 50 survived on the *Thielbek*.

I received a detailed report that Sonja looks very well and feels well. She had survived spotted typhus. I am anxiously waiting to receive a letter from her.

I must finish because the auto is leaving [with the letter].

With kisses,

Your Judel

In 1944, my mother, Sonja, was taken to Germany; as mentioned, while the men went on to Dachau, the women were taken to the Stutthof concentration camp. There, my mother was the chief nurse in the camp hospital. She always cared about her appearance, washing her few clothes every night after a twelve-hour shift, and she always looked clean, as reported later by surviving inmates. My mother showed great courage, staying in the operating room and doing her job while bombs were falling around the hospital. Once, half the staff was killed by a direct hit on the shed they were hiding in, while the operating room remained intact.

When the war came close to its end, on orders from Berlin, the women of the camp were evacuated and eventually placed on a number of barges, two of which ended up being anchored to the larger freighters in the Baltic Sea.[10] When the Allies dropped a bomb on the barge my mother was on, a part of it broke off and sank; the rest was on fire. My mother told me that she was wounded by a piece of shrapnel and lying unconscious on the burning barge when a German navy hospital ship pulled alongside it, lifting some of the remaining women, including my mother, onto the hospital ship. A German naval surgeon operated on her onboard the ship and saved her life.

$\sim$

---

10 The barges, Vaterland and Wolfgang, were anchored to the *Cap Arcona* and the *Thielbek*.

Here is my mother's first letter to my uncle in Africa, followed by a short note from me as well:

October 26, 1945

My Dear Samuel and Ann!

You cannot imagine my happy excitement today. I have just read your letter and I am immediately writing a reply. You cannot imagine what it means for a person who had no hope whatsoever to ever speak to you. Judel and I often used to say that you, dear Samuel, would not even know where our remains are.

My dear ones, if you only knew how many deaths, and how many types of deaths, were stalking us every day for the last four years, then you might understand my excitement today. And then you would also understand how much luck was required to crawl out of this bloodbath with life intact.

I am scared to speak about my luck, especially, on finding, thank God, my whole family. Unfortunately, very few families remained intact....

I have already been with my family for four weeks. I did not have the slightest idea where they were for fifteen months, and judging by what I saw in those fifteen months in the concentration camp, I could not even hope to find anyone. My despair went so far that I tried everything I could to commit suicide. For what good is life to me when in one minute everything that was dear to me and loved — my whole family — was taken from me. But fate wanted it otherwise, and when fate decides to intervene, we humans cannot change anything.

You cannot understand, my dear ones, how happy you should be that God protected you from all that.

During the fifteen months that we did not see each other, we changed considerably. Of course, our dear son is an exception — he is the only one who improved. Youth, of course, responds differently than age. I nearly did not recognize Elly. He is very tall and well-developed physically and mentally. I could say many good things about him, but I am afraid that you will laugh at me, thinking that only a mother talks like that. But he is really a mensch and I am very proud of him. Particularly because the Kazet [Concentration Camp] *has not corrupted him. Judel has aged a bit, but we must be happy and satisfied with the way things are. My dear brothers also turned quite grey. My sister-in-law and I are keeping well, considering the severe wounds we experienced, apart from all the other travails. Our only trouble now is that my brother's little daughter* [Shulamit, or Dalia] *is still not with us. We saved her from the annihilation of the children by leaving her with Lithuanian friends in Kovno. To retrieve her presents serious difficulties and this worries us greatly.*

My dears, I must tear myself away from sharing with you, for the letter will get too heavy, but I wish so much to speak to you. I haven't even started yet and I am forced to finish.

Try, our dears, to write in detail about yourselves, how you live, how your health is. You write very little about yourselves in this letter. We are all still in a half-lethargic sleep. One begins to wake up a little, and one begins to consider where one stands in the world. We are now like newborns who need to start life from the beginning. In the meantime, we are a bit too old for a whole new life, but one can do nothing about that. One must get a grip on oneself.

To sit now in Germany and live on German hospitality is a nice irony of life. But not for long. What we should do and what we should undertake we are not certain, for, as you, Samuel, wrote, the gates are locked for us everywhere, and our situation, after all that we survived, is desperate. But we must not worry — we are alive and that is the answer.

Keep well and healthy, my dear ones, and write to us soon. That is, for us, our greatest joy.

Your Sonja

Dear Uncle Samuel, dear Auntie Ann,

I really do not know where to start my letter, after an interruption of almost five years. There is so much to tell and so little space! What we have been through is so strange, so incredible, that soon I will look upon it as a dream and will not want to believe that I lived through it. One needed so much luck, mazel. *The life of each one of us hung on a hair; death was not in our hands but in front of our eyes, so one must become a fatalist and believe in blind luck.*

I have little space; Mother and Father wrote a lot. Hopefully we will meet.

You are kissed by,
Your Elly

The Drive to Get Out

After my mother and aunt Mary came to us in St. Ottilien, they still needed to recover. At some point in 1946, Aunt Mary travelled across borders illegally to get into Lithuania to find her daughter, Dalia (Shulamit), my little cousin who was taken out of the ghetto in a rucksack. She brought Dalia back to us in Germany. When she arrived, I was so thrilled that I shed tears. I would take her for walks and play with her. At first, she did not know who I was and why I was hugging her. We had to teach her Yiddish again — she had completely forgotten it and spoke only Lithuanian. Dalia has a special place in my heart.

We stayed in the area of St. Ottilien from May 1945 to May 1947. After spending six months in hospital, we went to live in the nearby village of Geltendorf, where the locals had to accommodate some Jewish displaced persons. We got rooms with a farmer who had a three-level house. My mother and father had one room and I had an attic room. Father became the *Jüdische Bürgermeister*, Jewish mayor, of Geltendorf, placing people in homes and dealing with complaints.

One day, a son of the farmer came back from the war on crutches. He had been in the Wehrmacht, a soldier in the regular army. They had another son, whom they did not expect to see again, they said. One day he came back, too. He had been in the SS! Who knows what he had done, where he had served. He always greeted us politely, but never spoke a word to us. We could never forget that we were under the same roof as a former SS man.

My parents were writing letters to our family in Africa, asking if they could get us out of Germany. These were moving, emotional pleas. When my uncle Samuel Gotz died in South Africa in 1983, I received several cartons of Yiddish books that he had left for me. At the bottom of one carton was an envelope addressed to me, inside of which were letters and a telegram. To my amazement these were all the letters my parents had sent to Samuel after liberation in Germany, before we immigrated to Africa and were united with him. I have included a few of the letters in my narrative at the appropriate place, as they describe my parents' desire to get out of Germany better than I can. All these letters are historical documents and describe vividly how desperate the lives of Holocaust survivors were after the war, how the world refused to accept us as refugees.

My parents were not only desperate to get out of Germany and start life anew somewhere, they were also concerned about my future. People suggested various countries to move to, but all — including America and Canada — appeared closed to Jews. We were writing to relatives in Palestine, but it was still under the British mandate, so there was no real chance of getting there. The British refused to allow Jews to enter, and we would soon hear stories of people being turned back or, worse, incarcerated. We applied to immigrate to some South American countries, but queues were long and nothing appeared to be moving.

I began to think again that I wanted to go to university and study engineering. But I wasn't going to go back to school in Germany with thirteen-year-olds when I was seventeen. At some point, I moved out of the village of Geltendorf to a large DP (displaced persons) camp in Landsberg am Lech, in Bavaria. I was assigned a room with three other Jewish men.

I had to determine which subjects I most needed to matriculate from high school. The most important to me was mathematics. I went outside the camp to the Landsberg high school and I asked the administration for the name of the teacher who taught math in the higher grades. They gave me the name of the teacher, Fraulein Blumenthal, and I asked for her address. Reluctantly, they gave it to me. I went to her house and knocked on her door. A middle-aged woman opened the door, saw a stranger standing there and looked worried.

"I am here to ask you to give me private lessons in mathematics. I need your help," I said. She started to tell me how busy she was at the school and how it would be hard for her to find the time. Then I asked her whether she had ever travelled to Munich by train during the war. She confirmed that she had. I asked whether she had noticed, at a point where the train travelled around a valley, the camp below. She said she had seen the camp and that the people looked so poor and thin. I told her that I was in that camp and then said, "I have suffered a great deal in your country, at the hands of your people. I think you should do this for me. I will only come twice a week, and I will pay." She invited me in and eventually asked me about my life story. I saw how moved she was by what she heard. She told me she would do her best to help me and that I didn't need to pay. But I decided I would pay her with coffee and chocolates, which the local people could not get. About eight months later, she had taken me straight through to matriculation level.

During this time, I also became interested in the history of art. I met a former university art professor, and I made a deal with him — coffee for lessons. I told him I had limited time — he had to take me from ancient to modern in four months. I went to the Catholic churches in Bavaria, and I saw distinctive styles of art; some reminded me of Greek and Roman myths, while others were entirely Christian, but in various styles. I got a good overview of Greek and Roman sculpture and architecture from the professor. Then I stopped, as I got busy with my other studies, especially in physics and chemistry.

I also went to check out the ORT school in the DP camp, which had just opened under the management of Mr. Jacob Oleiski. He was the original director of the ORT in Kovno and was also the founder of the Fachschule, the trade school that I had attended in the ghetto. Mr. Oleiski lived in Munich but often came to Landsberg and other places where he established schools. He did an exemplary job of setting up classrooms and workshops. Even in Landsberg, he had the gift of persuasiveness and the ability to find practical solutions to social problems. There were so many youths that had missed their school years and now needed practical training to prepare them for life.

When I walked into the school I was informed that a class for radio mechanics was starting that morning. My roommate Zamik Rubenchik and I attended the class for three days. The instructor opened an electronic tube and showed us the insides. He explained the basic principles of radio reception and transmission, how sound is attached to a radio wave and detached in the receiver. It was fascinating, and we wanted to learn more, so Zamik and I signed up for the course. We would graduate with a diploma as a qualified radio mechanic after eleven months.

Our classmates were all survivors of concentration camps — all young Jewish boys below the age of twenty. Our instructor, Mr. Albrecht, a German electrical engineer, was a good teacher. He gave us the minimum amount of math required to understand the construction of a radio receiver, electrical theory, high frequency and so on. I really began to enjoy the lessons and started to think that I would aim for electronic engineering rather than mechanical, which was my original plan. Every day I learnt something new I could marvel at.

We were beginning to build our own radio receiver from scratch. But it was difficult to find parts, which we had to supply ourselves. One problem presented itself early on when we couldn't find transformers for our radio sets. I discovered dozens of discarded transformers on a pile of waste outside a bombed-out factory, and when I tested a few I realized they were burnt out. I decided to try to rewind the burnt-out wiring. I carefully took apart one transformer and slowly unwound the many hundreds of turns — winding the wire onto another bobbin. After a while I came across the point where the wire had burnt out. I carefully soldered the two ends of broken wire, covered it with insulation and rewound the whole coil again. The transformer worked as good as new!

It was a very tedious process, so I constructed a winding machine, with a turn counter, by using simple parts. From a book I learnt how to calculate the number of turns required for each transformer. I opened a little workshop in my room for rewiring these transformers, which I sold or gave away to my classmates. I was in business!

I can never forget an incident that occurred in our class. There was one student who was totally uncommunicative; he didn't talk to anybody. I don't know what he had been through in the war. He had no family at all and he was totally closed off. All the students were working intently on their projects when, suddenly, his radio began to work. He was the first one to get a sound out of the radio. Everyone crowded around him, patting him on the back, congratulating him, and for the first time, I saw him smile. He had created something! A light came on in his eyes. From that day on he began, in a guarded way, to come back to life, talking to us. I realized then that knowing how to do something well has healing qualities.

The young people in the DP camp organized social activities and dances. Zamik and I were going out with two sisters. Clara, the younger sister, was a jolly girl with lots of personality. She liked to dance but I didn't have a clue how to, and I was constantly stepping on her toes. So, on the quiet, I went to a dance studio in town. I told the instructor that I wanted to learn but I didn't have a partner. He told me that I didn't need a partner, nor did I even need music. He taught me, "one, two, three, turn, step, step, step." That's how I learned to dance. Marching around the room, I learned the steps for every dance. Then he turned on a gramophone, and I was surprised to find I could dance! Now the question was — could I do it with a partner? One day I took Clara on a mysterious visit into town to that studio, and I proved to myself that the classes really worked. Clara was thrilled. I started to love dancing and became quite good at it. I am especially fond of the tango.

During all this time I was studying on my own and still trying to find out how to get into university. The Jewish organizations in Munich were starting to deal with students' requests for education. I went there and asked how to get into the engineering school at the university. They told me that the university was establishing a special committee of professors to examine students' readiness to enter university since none of the students had documents of matriculation.

I applied to be examined. On the appropriate day, I saw a crowd of applicants milling about. I got a number and then had to wait for several hours before my turn came. In the meantime, I spoke to some people as they came out from the oral exam. Some said it was very difficult and felt dejected because they were unable to answer the questions. Finally, my turn came. The interview was conducted in German by five examiners. They started with math, very simple questions about equations. As soon as they realized that I knew an answer, they cut me off and asked the next question, at the next level. In a few minutes, they determined my math knowledge. Then they moved to physics — in about twenty minutes they moved through all the physics to matriculation level. There were a few questions in chemistry, which I did not answer too well, and they were finished.

A brief time later I discovered that out of 146 students only about thirty had been approved — and I was one of them! They told me I would get a letter and that I should prepare myself. I was supposed to start in September, the fall of 1946. I was excited to study electronics. I didn't know how I was going to make it financially, but I would face that later.

However, my plans of going to university in Munich were soon thwarted. But I hadn't been looking forward to living in Germany and going to university with Germans anyway.

First Testimony

On January 4, 1947, I wrote the following testimony in Yiddish to the Central Historical Commission (CHC) in Munich[11]:

What experience in the Kovno ghetto left the deepest impression on me: As we know, the Kovno ghetto initially consisted of two parts: the so-called "large ghetto" and the "small ghetto." The large ghetto was the former Jewish neighbourhood, a densely built-up area, while the small ghetto consisted for the most part of detached houses and villas. Therefore the (Jewish) ghetto administration decided to set up a hospital for contagious diseases in that section. This hospital was very important for our ghetto because in our over-crowded living conditions, an infected person had to be isolated immediately.

We lived next to this hospital. For several days there were unconfirmed rumours that did not bode well. Finally, on Saturday, October 4, 1941, it began. At daybreak, men on their way to work were sent back home. Through the dense fog on the market square across the

---

11 The CHC was part of the Central Committee of Liberated Jews in the American Zone of Occupation in Germany, one of the first bodies to collect documents and evidence in order to start historical research of the Holocaust. Between 1945 and 1950, the committee represented displaced Jews, supporting various endeavours in education, culture, religion, law, emigration and employment.

road, silhouettes of people and cars slowly became visible. For three hours, from 5:00 a.m. to 8:00 a.m., the unknown gradually dawned on us. Through the window we could observe how the German soldiers and Lithuanian Hilfspolizei [the Lithuanian Auxiliary Police] (our good neighbours!) were forming groups, and at 8:30 a.m. the deafening bang of a rifle butt on our door and the shouts of "Get out!" echoed through our house. With small bags on our backs, the sign of the eternal wandering Jew, we went out to the market square. Passing the hospital, we noticed that it was under guard and saw terrified faces looking out at us from the windows. With cold blood in our veins, no longer able to think, but with a sense of foreboding, we walked, or rather were driven, across the bridge over the "Aryan" street that connected the small ghetto to the large ghetto. We went to friends.

Suddenly, there came a whisper, immediately followed by shouting from every direction: "The hospital in the small ghetto is on fire! And trembling voices added, "The patients were not allowed to leave."

I do not remember how I got to the roof on the neighbouring house. I only remember seeing smoke billowing out of the building across the street, flames like red snakes sticking their heads out of the windows and licking the roof.... My heart stopped, and one thought kept hammering at my brain: People are being burned alive in there! One horrifying image after another was conjured up by my imagination, which was reality, and reality mixed with fantasy on my forehead drenched in cold sweat. I felt that if I did not get down from the roof at once, I would soon be picked up from the ground. I climbed down, hid in a corner, and thought, and thought....

A week later, going back to fetch what was left of our plundered belongings, we were forced to pass the place where the hospital had stood. The black chimney stared at me silently. The remaining water pipes looked like outspread hands. To me the hands seemed to be signalling, the foundations recounting, and the black chimney bearing witness to the terrible suffering, the faces distorted by pain, and the screams heard by no one....

These were the methods employed by the German civilization (I am deliberately using the word civilization, not culture, because they are two completely different concepts) to protect people from infectious diseases!

The doctor on duty, two nurses, and all the patients — people who, for the most part, would have regained their health in two or three weeks — were burned alive.

There was a trade school in the ghetto where boys and girls learned a trade. I studied in that school. On one occasion the students were given the topic [to write about]: "What experience has had the most profound impact on me." What I wrote then is the same as what I am writing now.

Now, after the concentration camps, after all the terrible suffering, when I consider what has had the most profound impact on me over the past five years, it is the image of the patients and the doctors being burned alive.

The Wheel of Fate

My parents were still writing letters to our relatives and were still desperately trying to get us out of Germany. We asked the authorities about going to Eretz Yisrael (the Land of Israel) or to Australia or Africa, but it all looked hopeless. And then we unexpectedly received documents to fill in to go to Southern Rhodesia, where my uncle was working hard to get us in. The papers were just for the three of us, my parents and I, not for my mother's three brothers and families. This presented a difficult decision for my mother — whether to part with her family — which is clear from this letter to my uncle Samuel in Southern Rhodesia.

January 29, 1947
Dear Ann and Samuel!

Finally, after much effort and waiting, we have completed the necessary papers. Until last week there was no English consul, and we wanted to do everything the way you, Samuel, asked. That is why it took so long. In the end, when everything was ready, we could not obtain postage stamps to send it off. Finally, a friend who receives stamps from his relatives had pity on us and helped us out, may it be in a lucky hour!

We have become very impatient lately. Being in the cursed Germany, one can lose peace of mind and patience, bearing in mind our past. We are sitting here and seeing with our own eyes how they are getting stronger by the minute, and we are getting weaker every minute.

Although to separate myself from my dear brothers would be terrible for me, I would not remain here for another minute if I had the chance to leave Germany. I would run in the middle of the night, and not because of myself, God forbid, but because of Elinka. At thirteen years of age he was, without knowing why, locked up behind barbed wire and faced death constantly until age seventeen. That is not a small matter. The single thought that he may again have to suffer from these murderers drives me crazy. He is such a good person. He is very hard-working. With his youthful energy, he made up for what the terrible five years have taken from him. He has already dreamt up his way and aim in life, but to reach it he must leave Germany. If we are here, I have no peace. I know how hard it is to get out of here, almost hopeless, but I will not give up hope. Perhaps you will succeed in doing it. Until now we have been lucky in many disastrous situations. Why should I not hope now! I don't want to thank you for what you are doing for us. If it will be our fate to see you, I will do it personally.

Hearty greetings to you, my dear ones, and kisses from me and my whole family.

Your Sonja

But we didn't go to Rhodesia. What happened was that my uncle Tanchum found out that Norway was offering to take six hundred Jewish survivors. Our family — my three uncles, my aunts Nata and Mary and my cousin Dalia — decided to apply, since all our attempts to go elsewhere had failed. My parents and I had to decide whether to wait for the papers we had filled in for going to Rhodesia or go with my mother's family to Norway. Since we heard nothing for a long while after sending off the papers for Africa, we suspected that something had gone wrong, that perhaps the papers were lost, and a decision was required urgently.

People thought it was crazy for us to go to Norway, to the "polar bears." We didn't really know much about Norway. We read what some travellers to Norway wrote, that Norway didn't have jails and the people there didn't lock their houses. They said it was an amazing country with wonderful people. We were concerned, however, that Norway was close to the Soviet Union. We wanted to be farther away from the country known as the "White Bear." But after sitting and waiting for two years without hope, we applied, and then we accepted the offer to go to Norway.

The Norwegian government did the paperwork quickly, unlike other countries that took years to give papers. Within three weeks we were ready to travel. We had to go through medical tests with the UNRRA doctors and fill out all kinds of paperwork. In May 1947, we boarded a Norwegian ship at the Port of Bremen. On the ship we had to wear lifejackets because there was a risk of the ship hitting a mine. I think we spent two nights on the ship.

We arrived in the morning in the Oslofjord at Halden. When the ship approached the harbour, we could see a big crowd of people, and we soon heard shouting — we were surprised to find that they were there for us! The citizens of Halden began throwing us oranges and chocolates. We found out later that these were all rationed goods. There were trucks waiting to load us and our luggage, and we were driven to the Ystehede Camp in Halden, where there were rooms waiting for us. There, we were received by a quiet older gentleman named Rector Olden, a Quaker and former director of a high school.

There was a great shortage of housing in Norway at the time, since the German army, while retreating from Northern Norway, burnt down thousands of houses, but space for all of us was secured. In one long building every family got an apartment or rooms with a common front porch. Each place was fully furnished.

There was a communal dining room where three meals were provided for the refugees every day. Whale meat was a common food for Norwegians, but our people couldn't get used to the taste, and they stopped serving it. Although we were all Jews, we came from different countries with different customs. There were many Hungarian and Polish Jews, and we were the only ones from Lithuania.

One Friday, the Polish Jews offered to take over the kitchen to cook fish. The first time they cooked the fish, the Hungarians were disgusted. "What, you put sugar in fish?! We can't eat that." The next week the Hungarians cooked the fish. The Polish Jews ran out of the dining room shouting, "Fire brigade! We're burning!" There was too much pepper and paprika for them. They didn't ask us Litvaks what kind of fish we liked. Eventually the cooking was left to the Norwegian staff — neutral territory!

Now my parents had to tell the relatives in Africa the surprising fact that we were suddenly in Norway. Here are the letters they wrote:

May 15, 1947, Ystehede, Norway
Dear Uncle Isaac, dear Hertze,

You will surely be surprised to see the place where my letter comes from. I must say truthfully that for us the arrival here in Norway came so surprisingly fast that it is hard for us to believe that we are all here. That is, me with my family, my brothers-in-law, sisters-in-law and the little child, saved from the murderers' hands, we are all out from the borders of the bloodied German earth.

It all happened like so: From my last letter, you knew that we were preparing the papers which you, dear Hertze, had sent us, to immigrate to Africa. We were kept busy preparing photos, birth certificates, marriage certificates, etc. But I must tell you that deep in our hearts, considering some facts about the people who had long ago completed these necessary formalities yet were still sitting in Germany, despite the excellent connections that they have, well, deep in our hearts we doubted very much whether we would be able to emigrate from Germany soon....

Apart from that, last year my brother Samuel sent me applications to fill out for immigration to Rhodesia. I fulfilled all formalities at the British consulate, sent off the papers to Samuel and heard nothing further. It is very possible that my letters to him, or his letters to me, were lost. Similar cases were reported by many of my friends. The possibility of going to Eretz Yisrael in a legal way is out of the question for the next few years. (We cannot go illegally.) On the other hand, some people went to America, but we don't have anyone there, and without that there is no way. We registered for all countries where the governments have shown some willingness to take Jews, for example New Zealand, Canada, Holland, Norway. We did so because we have had enough of being in Germany. We cannot look any longer into the murderous faces of the Germans, although now they are wolves without teeth, or, it would be more correct to say, that they put on a sheep's skin now.

Many Jews registered for the countries I mentioned, except for Norway. There were only about 500–600 people registered because many do not wish to remain in Europe, and they fear the climate. Besides that, the closeness to the white bear.... Disregarding the advantages of the non-European countries, they had one big disadvantage: it is totally unknown how many people they will allow to come. Secondly, one does not know when.... Everyone wishes to get out of Germany as soon as possible. Norway did it fast and smoothly. Within about three weeks, everything was completed. We decided, although many conditions were put to us, and not easily accepted, like, for example, to be in a communal camp again for two months, where [due to the shortage of housing] we will have to live in barracks, but we were promised that the barracks will be solid and hygienic, and that we will be given jobs. And <u>here we are — in Norway</u>! We have no regrets, for firstly, we are no longer in Germany, and secondly, because the Norwegians are an exceedingly noble, honest, kind people. When we arrived in Norway they showed us such friendship, so much kindness (children and adults), that I cannot tell you how moving this was for us. For about two to three months the government will look after [us, supplying us] with food; we are taught the language (Norwegian), for the children there is a kindergarten, a school and so on. After that time, we will need to start building our own home. We understand that the beginning will be full of difficulties, mainly because Norway is a country that suffered from the war.

Some people, who have more assets, have already begun, little by little, to plan their future. This is not possible for us at present, due to our lack of resources. I therefore want to refer to your kind offer in previous letters to assist us, if possible. But I ask you not to do this through public organizations but simply through a bank, transmitting whatever funds you will find suitable in Norwegian kroner or British pounds.

So now, my dears, you can picture our situation. I also want to add that in five years we will receive citizenship. (That is the general law here.)

Dear Uncle, you mentioned in a previous letter that when we arrive in Eretz Yisrael, you would come to visit us. We would very much like to get to know you personally (I imagine you would like that too), so I ask that since that path was closed to us, not through our fault, that your decision to come could also apply to Norway. That would be the greatest event for us! We would have a great deal to share with you, dear Uncle. Incidentally, Norway is an incredibly beautiful country, because of both its nature and its people, and is known in the world as a beloved tourist haven. Please write to us with your thoughts on this. We also ask you to write in detail about your health. How are your eyes?

Dear Hertze, please let us know whether you received our detailed letter from St. Ottilien. How is your mother, your brothers and their families?

Well, keep well my dear ones, we wish you all the best and good health. Please write to us soon with more details about yourselves. The mail is better from here than from Germany. To you, Hertze, some hearty thanks again for all your efforts on our behalf. I would so much love to meet you and the families, to get to know you personally. Let us hope!

I kiss you heartily,
Your Julius

Dear Uncle,

I send my warmest greetings to you from Norway. Thank God, we are no longer in Germany. We inherited from our forefathers the description as a wandering people. The kind of wandering that fell to our generation is an altogether different kind of wandering. And who knows for how long still? Will Norway be our last stop? I don't know. In the meantime, we grabbed Norway like a drowning man grabs for a straw.

To depart Germany, the two years of our being there bothered us and gave us no rest.... After the six terrible years that we endured there was such a desire for some spiritual rest. We were hoping to find this rest amongst close and dear people. We were hoping that perhaps we will come to you, to Samuel, or to Palestine. Unfortunately, the experience of two years in Germany took all our hopes away. Hopelessly we observed how the world responds to our suffering. We understood that we must use all our own energy to get out from Germany. We did it! So now what? Now we need to gather up the small remainder of our energy and powers in a normal country, with good and lovely people, to try and fit into a foreign, new way of life. I want to hope that it will be all right.

I end my first letter from Norway with the wish that our future letters bring you much pleasure.

Keep well and healthy,

Your Sonja

Generally, we received a warm reception in Ystehede. People were anxious to help us and meet our needs. We even got monthly pocket money. All this was done under the direction of Rector Olden, who was a real jewel of a man. Once we were settled in, the government began providing daily lessons in Norwegian. University students, who I believe were volunteers, came to teach us. For me, the lessons were going too slowly. Adults are slow learners! I began to work energetically to learn Norwegian by reading the paper every day with a dictionary and by speaking to anyone who was willing to give me a little time. Within three months I was speaking Norwegian quite fluently.

The student teachers helped organize dances for us. There were many more men than women, and we asked the students how to invite more women. The Norwegian guys told us to just put up a notice that there's a dance, and they would come. Many did come, and we danced, but we couldn't really talk to them. The conversation was very shallow.

We all had Primus stoves in our rooms for boiling water for tea or coffee. We were supplied with a large drum of kerosene, but we needed to dispense it into smaller containers for the Primus stoves. Filling a container with a small opening from a drum was impossible. The kerosene would spill on the ground, creating a fire hazard, so I made a funnel for the family to use. Since everyone needed a funnel, I set up a small workshop to make them from a piece of metal roofing that I found.

I grew friendly with Rector Olden, and I discussed with him my dream of studying engineering. He discovered that I knew very little organic chemistry, which I would need to pass matriculation in Norway. Since he was trained as an organic chemist, he offered me daily lessons using a Norwegian textbook. Sometime later, he told me that a friend of his in Oslo had asked him how she could help the Holocaust survivors. He recommended me to her so that I could study and work in a city, and I received a warm letter from her inviting me to come and live with her and her son, who was a little younger than me.

Agnes Broch was an astronomer who was working as an actuary in an insurance company. Her husband, an officer in the Norwegian army, had been killed during the German occupation of Norway. She was a most gracious, warm woman and she treated me with great kindness. I shared a room with her son, Tom. He helped me with Norwegian and I helped him with math, which was not his favourite subject. One thing about Tom that was hard for me to get used to: at night, even when it was freezing, he kept all the windows wide open. He assured me it was very healthy and told me that when he and his friends wanted a bit of fun, they would find these open windows and throw snowballs into the room. That was not something I wanted to experience!

I decided to study at night school. My focus was admission into the Norwegian Institute of Technology in Trondheim, which was where engineers were trained in Norway. In the meantime, I would look for a job. I passed by a radio workshop, went in and showed the boss my ORT certificate, which didn't mean much to him. I said he could try me out for two weeks without pay and then decide if I could do the job. After two weeks, he paid me and hired me permanently.

My boss specialized in car radios, which was a challenge in Norway at the time; the Germans, during the occupation, had demanded that all short-wave reception parts be ripped out of car radios to prevent listening to faraway "enemy" broadcasts. Now people wanted to get wider reception from England/Europe on short wave. I calculated how to make a coil that could tune in to these other frequencies, and after some experimentation I managed to achieve it. My boss could then offer to reinstall all his clients' short-wave reception. He was very pleased with me. In the evening, when everyone left the workshop, he told me in a conspiratorial tone that he would pay me additional cash "under the table," but that I must keep it private. The term at first was confusing to me, its meaning hard to imagine. I glanced furtively under the table, then I guessed what he meant.

~

In Oslo, I was working and attending night school twice a week, but I worried that it would take years to graduate. Matriculation in Norway required good knowledge of English, French and German, with exam essays in two of these and a translation test for the third. In addition, good knowledge of three Norwegian dialects was required: Standard Norwegian, Old Norwegian (like Old English) and New Norwegian (Nynorsk). The latter was an attempt to unite all Norwegian dialects into one new language. Of all these languages, I knew only German and some Norwegian. I also found out that the engineering school only accepted a few of the very best students in the country, so my chance of getting in appeared limited, although Rector Olden had kindly written a letter to the university urging them to consider my acceptance when I was ready.

I began to have doubts that I would ever achieve my aim to graduate as an engineer. My parents were also having difficulties — after three months in Norway, our government assistance ended, and we needed to find housing in a city so that my parents could find work, but there was still an acute housing shortage in Norway. My father wrote detailed letters to his uncle Isaac in Johannesburg, asking for financial assistance to settle down in a city in Norway so that I could attend school and he could seek a better job. The reply was that it was not permitted to send money out from the country, but that if we could come to Africa, he would make sure I could attend university.

When the offer arrived to go to Africa, coupled with Uncle Isaac's offer to assist me in attending university in Johannesburg, I was more than willing to move again. In the meantime, my father heard from his brother Samuel, who lived in Bulawayo, Rhodesia, that he had finally received permission for us to come to Rhodesia!

There were many stressful barriers and frustrating complications around obtaining visas, exit papers, entry permits and other documents before my parents and I could finally leave Norway for Africa. It was hard for us, and especially for my mother, to leave the rest of our family, with whom we had been through so much, to go to my father's family in Africa. Also, we had agreed to stay in Norway at least five years, and now we were asking the government to release us from the promise. At the beginning of August 1947, my mother wrote to Uncle Samuel that, "Our mood is a heavy one.... We are stuck here between heaven and earth. We must, however, be happy with everything and not lose hope. We have enough hard, terrible years behind us and we have learned much."

Two weeks later she wrote to Uncle Samuel:

It is difficult for me to leave my brothers.... In the worst days they were always there, ready to help us. If not for my brothers, my family and I would not have been able to succeed in the hard, bitter battle of the recent years. The terrible past has bound us all tighter to each other. Before, I would have said that I cannot live without my family. Now, I cannot say it. For a whole year I did not know whether my husband and child were alive, and yet I lived.... By suffering together with them here, my brothers say, I would not help them. Apart from that, I am thinking about our dear son. Uncle promised that he would have the opportunity to study. To give him this possibility would make him happy. And tell me, my dears, who, if not Elly, has a right to happiness? A child who has such a terrible past behind him. A child who at thirteen years old was locked up and condemned to hunger, pain and slavery for so many years. My heart bleeds every time I think of it. I feel guilty for him. I would so much like my guilt about him to be forgiven by making him happy in his life, but I am alone, without assistance, unable to give it to him. That is why I want to do everything possible that is in my power to do.

We soon discovered that we could not obtain tickets to go to Africa by ship for at least two years — all passage had been booked by the thousands of others trying to emigrate. Many letters ensued between my parents and my uncles Samuel and Isaac, and Cousin Hertze, trying to figure out whether we could travel by plane, an extremely costly undertaking at the time. My mother wrote to Uncle Isaac:

The last six years have damaged us physically and spiritually, and we would surely not be able to fight any longer, if not for our son. We would also not have dared to trouble you so much, and to expect so much of you, if it had not been about our child.... We will do everything in our power to make good for our daring to bother you so much.

Eventually, my uncle Isaac was able to send us airline tickets. On October 7, 1947, my mother wrote to Uncle Samuel:

Exciting Beginnings

The day before leaving Oslo we went to a hospital to greet a newborn — Uncle Tanchum and Nata's daughter, Liv — our first Norwegian-born relative, my dear cousin. The next day we went to the airport to fly to Africa.

It was, for all three of us, our first flight. It was a four-engine propeller aircraft — a Douglas DC-4 Skymaster. We took off with snow falling on the ground in Oslo, and we landed many hours later in the warmth of Tunis, Africa. The smell of oranges and lemons filled the air — it was amazing. We took off again and flew overnight, landing in the rain in Kano, Nigeria, at breakfast time. We were fascinated as we watched the raindrops evaporate as they hit the ground. We sat at long tables, and behind us stood black waiters — we had never seen black people before.

Our next stop was Elizabethville, Belgian Congo (now called Lubumbashi, in the Democratic Republic of the Congo), where my mother's relative Teddy Koton met us. My mother had last seen him as a child in Kovno, when she took him to the train station to begin his journey to America to join his older siblings. He had been orphaned, and no one from his family was left in Lithuania. Now he was an officer in the US army and was stationed in Elizabethville, and he was very touched to see my mother again. Teddy took us for dinner at the Elizabethville Zoo. It was dark as we sat next to a metal fence, but when my eyes adjusted I saw a huge crocodile not more than ten feet away from me. I'd never seen one before. The experiences, each the first of its kind in my life, were piling up!

We stayed overnight in a hotel, and in the morning we took off for South Africa. Our plane landed at Palmietfontein Airport outside Johannesburg. We were greeted very warmly by my father's uncle Isaac, as well as by a large group of extended family that we had never met before.

On the way from the airport into the city, one of our new-found relatives, Hertze Missulawin, who was driving, lost his way and needed to ask for directions. He leaned out of the window and called out to someone, "Hey, John, which way to Jo'burg?" I was surprised and asked how he knew this man. "I don't know him. All blacks are John," he replied. This was the first of many cultural surprises I encountered in South Africa and Rhodesia.

We were driven to an elegant home where the table was set with tasty food and drinks. There was a lot of laughter and chatting. Fortunately, we had a common language and could communicate in Yiddish. Many of the Jews in South Africa had emigrated from Europe both before and after World War I — up until the 1930s. Thousands had come from Lithuania and had successfully integrated into the local community.

We expected to be asked about our experiences during the war years. My father started to explain what had happened in the ghetto. However, it soon became clear that this was not a topic that people wanted to discuss. My father was told, "Julius, don't talk about it. You'll only upset yourself." We realized that their concern was not to save my father from pain but to save themselves. We had a lot to tell, and we were willing to talk, but they were not willing to listen. When I realized how unwelcome our tales of suffering were, I decided to never talk about our experience again. And I didn't, for about twenty-five years.

We got the message that day, and later we realized that their reaction was not unique — the subject of the concentration camps and the killings was not generally acceptable talk. My father would still try to recount what we had been through, but I remained silent.

As we had been refused residence by the antisemitic government in South Africa, the National Party, we had to leave Johannesburg and continue our journey to Bulawayo in Southern Rhodesia. We were anxious to settle in our new country, but when we discovered that Bulawayo was about 850 kilometres from Johannesburg, we realized that we would have to travel by train for a full two days. Our previous experiences travelling by train had been fraught with danger and dread, yet this train journey filled me with amazement. For hours on end we travelled through semi-desert. All I saw was brown grass and scattered trees. In Europe, every few miles was a new town or village; here there were no towns or villages we could see, but whenever the train stopped, within a couple of minutes dozens of half-naked or poorly dressed black children would gather around the train, begging. Where had they come from? Everything was so unfamiliar to me. It was daunting and exciting at the same time.

Somewhere between Johannesburg and Bulawayo, in the open countryside, the train broke down, and we were stopped for about an hour. I jumped off the train and was amazed to see that the railway tracks stretched all the way to the horizon, in both directions. This gave me an indication of the size of the country we had come to, and the huge distances.

At the station in Bulawayo my father and his brother had a very emotional greeting. The last time I had seen my uncle Samuel was in 1936, when I was eight years old. Uncle Samuel had worked hard for two years to persuade the Rhodesian government to grant us permission to settle in Rhodesia.

Uncle Samuel and Aunt Ann had a small house with one extra bedroom for my parents and a couch in the living room for me. It was not an ideal arrangement, but it gave us an opportunity to acclimatize to this new way of life. With the help of the local Jewish community, we were soon able to move to more comfortable accommodations.

Once again, language was a huge barrier. English was a difficult language for me to master. I was puzzled by the rules of spelling, grammar and pronunciation. I immediately found a teacher from the local school to give me English lessons. To be accepted into a university I needed to pass the high school matriculation exam, which meant that I had to attend school for nine months to accumulate the credits required. The school year started in January, so I had about a month to prepare myself to start classes.

It was decided that I would do best in a technical high school and that is where I enrolled, in Grade 12. The headmaster of the high school was reluctant to take me in. I was a year or two older than the other boys, and I was an odd bird in this very conservative country. It was an all-boys school and all the students were white.

The relationship between whites and blacks was of great interest to me. Every white household had at least one black servant who lived in the backyard, in a small single room. Apart from the servants who lived in the white suburbs, the blacks lived in their own defined, segregated areas called "Locations." Later, the whole political situation changed dramatically, but in 1947 that was the accepted way of life for white people.

I acquired a bicycle to get to school and rode down the huge streets, wide enough for a wagon with oxen to do a 180-degree turn. At lunchtime I escaped from the noisy schoolyard and cycled to the beautiful local park to eat my lunch. The park was a luscious richness of palm trees shading bundles of every kind of African flower. Strelitzia flowers tilted their inquiring heads in the hundreds. I wish I knew the names of the countless other beauties there. The grass was constantly being sprayed with water to keep the green carpet lush in the burning heat of the day.

Palm trees were always my special love from afar, in Lithuania. As a kid, I loved the pictures of palm trees on stamps, and I used to dream of one day sitting under one. I found one little palm tree in the botanical gardens in Kovno, and a banana plant nearby, and I used to return there to admire them often. Now, in the Bulawayo park, I was in palm heaven!

I didn't know that leaving the school grounds was against the rules, so I was surprised when the headmaster called me to his office and asked me why I was leaving the school without permission. I told him, "I love to sit under a palm tree, and I look at all the beautiful flowers." He looked at me strangely and said, "All right, but be discreet."

The boys had some fun with me, too. Once, we had to study a Shakespeare sonnet, and there was nothing the boys hated more than poetry. When they read those beautiful words, it sounded to me like they were chopping wood. I said that aloud, so the boys shouted, "Okay, Gotz, so you read it!" So, with my broken English and terrible accent, but with all my heart, I read all fourteen lines of Shakespeare's famous sonnet "Shall I compare thee to a summer's day." The boys were literally rolling on the floor with laughter; even the polite teacher cracked a smile.

I had no trouble getting a passing mark in math, physics, drafting and German. I read an English newspaper every day with a dictionary at my side. And, wanting to be sure to pass the English exam, I went for private lessons and wrote two compositions a week. My teacher would mark the errors with a red pencil, and I would go home and rewrite them. I worked very hard. I chose to write about current events, philosophy, book reviews, astronomy, relationships and even about my neighbour's dog. At the bottom of one essay the teacher wrote, "I admire and I despair." But I learned to write a simple English sentence whose structure was clear to me. I passed the final English exam with an A, and I passed German with distinction. I also learned to drive, although we did not own a car for a good while.

At the school, we had a cadets group, and everyone had to belong. Since Rhodesia was a British colony, everything was run by the rules of the British army. Officers came and lined us up, and we marched through the streets to the shooting range. We were instructed to march with our arms swinging. I felt embarrassed swinging my arms like a wild man. I glanced around, concerned about what my friends were thinking, and an officer reprimanded me.

When we got to the rifle range, I discovered that all my classmates knew how to use a rifle. Most of them had one of their own. I had to tell an officer that I had never fired a rifle and asked if he would kindly show me how to use it. He lay down on the ground next to me, explained everything very patiently, and I then fired the rifle several times with reasonable accuracy. I was very excited about this new skill. Later, when we had discussions with the officer about strategy on the battlefield, how to get out from the trenches and take an enemy position, I participated with interest.

I began exploring the countryside. The large hills of bare rock were sometimes a challenge to climb. Cecil Rhodes, the British Empire builder who led the occupation of Rhodesia for the British, is buried at Matobo, one such bare hill near Bulawayo. I came to love the many landscapes of Rhodesia. Depending on the season, they changed from lush to totally dry and yellow.

In Bulawayo, the Jewish community was small, but there was an active cultural life in this far corner of Africa. I joined the Zionist youth organization and made friends. My uncle Samuel was the chairman of several Jewish organizations and arranged lectures. Lecturers came from South Africa and Israel, and the reception was always warm and well attended. At a Jewish club, I learned to play snooker.

I was accepted into the circle of a Jewish family that had escaped from Hitler's Germany, and one of their daughters became a close friend of mine. This family was voraciously passionate about classical music. In addition to attending every possible local classical concert and criticizing it viciously after (the local standard of music was considered very low — they attended only for lack of better options), they held musical evenings at their home with great decorum. They had a vast collection of vinyl records and the best equipment on which to play them. A group of regulars, all refugees from Germany, attended the "concerts," and I was invited too. Everyone came dressed almost formally and sat absolutely still during the performance. Coughs were frowned upon; sneeze twice and you must banish yourself to another room. A typed program listing each musical number to be played, the conductors and main performers was distributed. After the concert, coffee was served in elegant, beautiful porcelain with some delicious cake baked by the hostess. During intermissions there was polite, learned discussion about the music that had just been heard, even criticism by the more knowledgeable members of the circle. A critic was never criticized in turn, but an even finer point might be brought up by another. In that company, I learned a good deal about classical music and later in life attended concerts with pleasure.

~

There was no university in Rhodesia, so I enrolled in the electrical engineering department at the University of the Witwatersrand (Wits), in Johannesburg. I departed from Bulawayo on the two-day train journey, full of anticipation and excitement, on my way to achieving my main goal in life!

My father's Uncle Isaac was true to his word and paid for my tuition and board. I moved into a rooming house that operated on absolute minimum standards, but it was located across the road from the university, and I could roll out of bed and be in class within ten minutes. This was a big plus for me, as I am not a morning person.

Every day, I thought about how lucky I was to have achieved my place there. I was a diligent student. I noticed that there was a group of five students who all sat at the front of the class and were serious about learning, so I attached myself to that group. We were always together, discussing the material, helping each other, going for lunch, talking politics. I made lifelong friends with two of them, Norman and John. Norman Morrison, a Jewish boy who was brilliant when it came to mathematics, later moved to the United States, obtained a doctorate and made significant contributions to engineering science. I treasure all the books he has written. We see each other when he visits Toronto, where his daughter Lisa and her family reside, and we always delight in each other's company. I also became close with John Blank. His parents, German Jews, escaped Germany during Hitler's rule, just in time. John also moved to the United States, and he worked as an engineer for General Electric. We always kept in touch. In 2017, when I heard the sad news that he was very ill, I flew to see him and his two wonderful sons, Steven and Dan. He passed away shortly after my visit.

Another member of our group became well known in the United States — Dr. Tingye Li, who worked for Bell Labs and developed the glass fiber optics communication technology. He was the son of the Imperial China ambassador in South Africa. It was a good group to be part of, and it helped me to learn successfully. I also fondly remember Professor Bozzoli, a wonderful teacher. One day he took me aside and asked about my past. When I told him my story, he was very moved, and he was always kind to me.

Each summer I returned by train to Bulawayo to be with my parents, and I worked in a radio workshop to earn money for my education. Uncle Isaac died after my second year at university, but by then I was earning enough from my summer job to complete the last two years of study.

After four years, in 1952, I graduated with a bachelor of science in engineering, specializing in electronics. My parents were present at my graduation and shared my happiness. I won a scholarship to study at a prestigious company in England, but when the authorities discovered I was not a British citizen and that I was a "stateless person," I was not eligible to accept the scholarship. Professor Bozzoli brought me the news with great regret.

I returned to Bulawayo. I had plans to hitchhike through Africa to Europe, but I saw that my parents were having a tough time financially. I then tried to find a job as an engineer, but Rhodesia had little industry and there were no jobs for me. I helped my parents open a bicycle store, and then I established a radio repair shop inside the store, which soon became successful. I began selling radios to the black population and then expanded the radio repair business by having two messengers on bicycles tour many stores in town to pick up radios for repair, returning them the following morning. I would do all the repairs at night and became very adept at doing them quickly.

One day I had an idea: The black population was the majority in town, and they lived in the poor parts of town, which had no entertainment at all. I applied to the municipality for permission to establish an open-air projection screen in one such "Location," to show free entertainment. Once I received permission, I began to plan to display advertising slides at night. That required that I go out to find advertisers from the local stores that were catering to this population. I had no money at all, so I insisted that the advertisers pay in advance for three months.

My father had no business experience in his life, yet he now became concerned with my business activities, that I was selling advertising without having any business yet. He warned me, "You are taking people's money without any business in sight! You will end up in jail and a disgrace to us all." I didn't listen — I was driven to achieve success, to build a successful business.

The advance payments that I collected from advertisers put some money in my bank account, so I purchased a used van and installed inside a large slide projector and a full record playing set-up, with amplifiers, a microphone and a loudspeaker on the roof. I did all my own installation since I had the skills.

Soon I was at the site of the screen every night, showing advertising slides. I hired a confident African man at the microphone who would speak about the advertising slides — as many locals could not read — and tell jokes to the merriment of the audience, who were standing around in the street. He spoke several local languages, so everyone in the crowd could understand him.

I remember one joke: "Hey, I was walking at night here, and a man comes over to me and asks for the time, so I look at my watch and tell him it's ten o'clock. Then he says — have you seen a policeman around here? — I say no, I have not. So, he pulls out a knife and demands I give him my watch!" The audience was rolling with laughter.

After a while I expanded my screens to five separate "Locations" in town, visiting each one once a week. Sometimes I had huge audiences, three thousand people sitting on a sloping hill, with the screen below in the valley and the projector van parked at the top of the hill.

I persuaded an advertising agency in Johannesburg to come and see my business. Two executives arrived in Bulawayo, and one night I took them to see my show. We were driving through unlit, bumpy streets in the poor part of town, and my guests became very worried. They locked the car doors and asked if it was safe to be there. I reassured them. Then we arrived at the top of the hill, and I invited them to come out and see the audience below. They could barely believe what they were seeing — several thousand people sitting on the ground and watching the presentations.

After that, I persuaded them to give me animated films with an ad at the end for Coca-Cola, and that became such a success that I started making films myself. I obtained a 16mm Paillard Bolex camera, read up on techniques and filmed local sports events. These became extremely popular, and people were asking for more of the same, which increased the value of my advertising sales. I also began to make primitive advertising films, including stop-motion films, where inanimate objects move, such as a spoon spreading out tea leaves on a table with the brand of the tea etched on the white cloth. My audience marvelled aloud at these films. I also approached the record companies and proved to them that by playing new records by local artists, I could really promote sales of these records.

I partnered with people who ran a newspaper that served the black population, and we outfitted two new vans, attaching electric generators, and sent them out with our advertising/entertainment programs to the outlying villages.

Then I had another plan for a business: sound recording. I opened a recording studio together with a Scottish engineer. We developed two kinds of activities: supplying amplifiers and loudspeakers for public events and recording music and speeches on vinyl records. My partner, Alistair, was an experienced recording engineer and had worked for the BBC in England. He was working for the local radio company, so it was a part-time business for both of us. I was in charge of finding business, and then we both worked on filling the orders. I was very good at fixing sound issues at public events by installing networks of small loudspeakers across a room so that everyone could hear. Our business became very successful.

I was busy day and night running several companies at the same time, and I discovered that I loved it! I became convinced that I could start any company I wanted if I had an original concept and an idea of how it might succeed. Since my parents had never been in business, I never received any useful background knowledge. Business was all new to me, and I learned as I went along.

～

It was not all work and no play for me though. I wanted to explore the country, its vast empty spaces, the mountains, the bush. I came to love the land and its peoples. I felt keenly the injustices done to black people, and I was embarrassed to be a white man and to be part of such an oppressive system, but I had to be careful about expressing my thoughts on these matters to local white people.

I joined a riding club and learned to ride horses, later leading groups of new riders through the bush. It is a wonderful feeling to go out riding through the countryside in the late afternoon, smell the smoke from village fires wafting through the air and see the sun setting slowly. These were magical moments that I remember fondly.

I also tried jumping on horseback. It is a special feeling when the horse bends its hind legs and takes a mighty jump upwards. I learned to stand up in the stirrups at that moment, as otherwise the mighty push from behind could send me flying forward over the horse's head!

I wanted to own a rifle. All my teenage years, I had guns pointing at me. Now I wanted to have one myself. There was very little paperwork involved for white people to obtain guns. I acquired a hunting rifle and a heavy revolver and learned to use them safely. I was thinking of learning to hunt, having read many books on famous African hunters.

In Bulawayo, I met a man who told me that he and his friend were planning to go on a crocodile hunt. I met his friend, Cecil, the leader, who was an experienced hunter, and he agreed to let me join. I helped them weld a boat from sheet iron. Including me, there were six men in the boat: the man who introduced me; Cecil the leader; an older man who had excellent eyesight and was known as a good spotter; and two other black African men who worked for Cecil.

Cecil was planning to become a professional crocodile hunter, and this was his first attempt to see if he could make it pay. Crocodile skin is considered one of the finest and best, being soft and durable. But only the skin on the belly has these qualities; the top skin is covered in bones that can deflect arrows and spears! Only the belly of the crocodile can be sold, and the value is assessed per inch of the width of the skin. The skins needed to be rubbed with salt for preservation, so we brought bags of salt with us.

We drove in Cecil's truck from Bulawayo to Victoria Falls, where we lowered our boat into the Zambezi River. Fifty kilometres upriver from the falls, the Zambezi is over a mile wide, with islands in some places. Many crocodiles were sunning themselves on the islands, but they disappeared as soon as we got close. In Africa, the crocodile has the reputation of being the meanest and the most ferocious of animals. It has earned a reputation as a people-eater, and in its presence caution and respect are always advised.

The only way to hunt crocodiles is at night, when they float in the river hunting for fish. Cecil wore a miner's powerful light on his head to scan the river. Crocodile eyes shine red when caught in the head-light; I was told that they have crystals behind their retina that reflect light and make their night vision possible.

Voices can scare away the crocs, but the engine noise did not bother them. Cecil sat in front and waved his arms to indicate which way to direct the boat. I steered the motor following his instructions. When he located a crocodile, he waved his hands up and down, which meant, "slow down." He lifted his double-barrelled .458 elephant gun, aimed one inch above the line of the eyes of the crocodile and fired at close range. Crocodiles have a valve in their throat that is closed when they are in the water. When shot, the valve opens involuntarily, and the crocodile begins to sink by taking in water, so we had to grab the croc as soon as the boat was on top of it. The bone in a crocodile's head is about three inches thick at the front, so even an elephant bul-let at close range does not always kill it, but just stuns it.

We shot three crocodiles that night and brought them back to our camping spot on the shore. Cecil's crew then skinned them and threw the remainder of the carcasses into the bush, away from the tents. In the morning, there was a huge cry coming up from where we had left the carcasses — a flock of vultures had descended to clean up. They were putting their heads inside the carcasses and coming up red with blood, and they were fighting with each other. Nature has its own laws. What a sight!

We also had the doubtful pleasure of meeting a female hippopota-mus head on, though it was her other end that we actually crashed into. She was sleeping while standing in the high reeds close to shore, and we didn't see her as we were steering the boat through the reeds. There are no brakes on a boat, and the prow hit her from behind in a very sensitive spot. With a mighty grunt, she threw herself sideways into the water, and the huge wave nearly tipped us over. We expected an attack, but none came. On another occasion, a male hippo took exception to our presence in his waters and swung his head against our boat. With his front tooth, he made a one-inch hole in our steel boat just below the waterline. Luckily, we were very close to shore.

One night, as I was guiding the boat and contemplating the half-moon shining on the dark water, a shot rang out and Cecil shouted, "Grab him before he sinks!" I stuck my hand in the water and grabbed the leg of a crocodile, holding on as best I could. Two of my mates grabbed its other leg and its tail. The others leaned toward the other side of the boat to prevent it from tipping over. We dragged the ten-foot crocodile into the boat.

I was at the engine, and the crocodile's head was beside my leg. I revved up the motor and we moved again. Then I felt something moving near my leg, so I picked up the flashlight and looked down. The crocodile's jaw was opening and closing right next to my leg! I shouted, "Cecil, he's moving!" Cecil told me to shoot the croc in the ear with my revolver. I carried a .45 on my waist, but I was afraid to shoot into that crocodile's ear in case the bullet went through his head and the boat as well. Cecil grabbed the gun from my reluctant hand and fired into the crocodile's ear. He said, "Nothing ever comes out of a crocodile's head on the other side!" The croc closed its jaw and lay still. I asked myself, Elly Gotz, what are you doing here?

It was an exciting week for me. We shot about fourteen crocodiles, some of them fifteen feet long. We hunted wild ducks and ate them for dinner, while the mosquitoes ate us. In daytime, we relaxed and fished. I mounted a half-pound of crocodile meat on a huge fishhook and flung it far out into the river, and a moment later I had a large tigerfish at the end of my line. It fought me for a long time before I pulled it in. I still have the photograph of myself in a bush hat, un-shaved and grinning, with the large fish hanging by my side. That photo captures a very happy moment for me.

Fulfilling Love and Dreams

For the first five years after graduating from university, I was mighty busy running several businesses at the same time, riding horses, climbing mountains, hunting, reading, making friends, going out ballroom dancing, exploring the countryside. I also tried to sign up for flying lessons, but my mother screamed at me, "You survived Dachau and now you want to kill yourself?!" So out of respect for my mother's fears, I delayed learning to fly. A friend took me flying in a Tiger Moth airplane, and we did a "dead loop" — flying in a full circle vertically, upside down — I loved it!

Then I began thinking that I would soon be thirty and that it was time to find a woman I could love all my life. I began looking with purpose. It took me a while, yet I had an enjoyable time searching.... One day, while visiting Johannesburg on business, I called a telephone number someone had given me for a blind date. People kept giving me telephone numbers — they must have felt I was in need. I called Esme Cohen. She was away in Europe. No problem — I called again a few weeks later, and Esme was back in town. I invited her for tea in the afternoon. I had tickets for the following night for a Flamenco dance troupe that was visiting from Spain. I always loved Flamenco dancing. Now I had to decide whom to invite. After having tea with Esme, I had no doubt whatsoever and invited her to the show. I was very happy to meet such a delightful woman.

After that, things happened very fast. Soon we had dinner togeth-er and I told her that when we got married we would go to Europe — across the whole of Europe! She pointed out that I had not asked her yet. She thought I may have been drunk that night, but I confirmed my intentions the following day.

We got married in March 1958. I was totally, totally in love. It was the first time in my life I had wanted to get married, and it happened! I was totally happy. Now, at age ninety, I want to confirm that I am still in love with Esme.

Esme's parents were from Lithuania and had left after World War I. Her mother, Hilda, was born in Kaunas, where my mother and I were born. Her father, Abram, was from a small town called Pashvetin, very close to my father's town of Šiauliai. One day our fathers were discussing their childhoods when my father remembered being in a field outside his town when a primitive airplane landed there. Esme's father exclaimed, "I was there too!" The plane was a simple structure of wood and canvas flown by a grandson of Mendele Mocher Sforim — the writer of classic Yiddish literature. He was flying from Berlin to Moscow, while his mechanic was driving on the ground. He needed to land for a repair, and both our fathers were there as young boys to witness it. So our family connections go back a long way!

Esme moved to Bulawayo with me, and we worked together on making the stop-action advertising films. Some evenings she sat with me while I did the radio repairs. Once, I opened a large radio receiver and a small mouse ran up my arm to my shoulder, turned around and went back into the radio. I quickly closed the cover and sent it back with a note to please remove the mouse before sending it back to me for repair.

Esme's parents had been in business a long time, running a leather factory called Rand Leather Works Ltd. Esme's mother, Hilda, worked full-time alongside her husband, Abram, every day for many years. Later, their sons, Norman and Lew, joined in. Lew had graduated as a mechanical engineer, and after a stint in the mines joined the factory.

Norman became a skilled buyer and manager. Esme, after graduating with a degree in social sciences, used her skills as a salesperson in the plant. She went out with two heavy suitcases, carried by a member of the staff behind her, and visited the wholesalers in town. After initial amusement from the wholesalers, who had seldom seen a woman selling, she was taken seriously and was very successful. Her father had wanted to cut her commissions to discourage her from going to Europe on her own, but she had stood her ground and went off to Europe for a long visit. I met her just after her return.

Esme's brother Lew visited various exhibitions in Europe and collected some interesting information about the innovative technology of electronic welding of plastics. In 1952 the South African government had passed a new segregationist law and was seeking tenders to produce millions of plastic pouches for the black population to carry the hated passes, restrictive documents that gave the bearer permission to be in a certain district only. Of course, only black people had to carry these.

Lew worked out a price with the government without having laid his hands on the new equipment required to produce these pouches. It was a very bold move for the family, to accept this large order and give guarantees that they would deliver. Lew flew to Europe and ordered the machines and materials and began this new production facility on the second floor of the leather factory. They named the company Weldo Plastics. Esme's father told me that he did not sleep well the entire year. The risk was great, but Lew managed to produce the order on time and with decent quality.

After living in Bulawayo with Esme for a time, her family, who had always received me warmly, offered for me to come to Johannesburg and join the family business. My electrical engineering knowledge could be of use with all this electronic production equipment. It sounded very interesting to me, and we decided to make the move. I sold off my several small businesses and entered Weldo Plastics with great enthusiasm. I enjoyed talking to Esme's father in Yiddish about

Jewish events and issues. He spoke and wrote Yiddish well, even published letters in the Yiddish press. I soon felt at home in this family and comfortable in the business.

My parents were then living a more stable life, and I was less concerned about moving away from them to Johannesburg. My mother had learned English and started a factory for manufacturing women's clothes with a partner, and my father had a job as statistician in a large factory. They lived in their own house. My mother loved to experience new things, and she travelled whenever possible. She also had a dramatic bent and participated in theatre productions. She was a delightful storyteller — an event took on life when she told about it. Her letters to friends and relatives were admired and retained. In another time, she might have been a writer.

Weldo Plastics Ltd. quoted and received the second large order for the government pouches, so there was lots to do. I became familiar with the machines, learned to repair them myself and later worked on developing more efficient ways to produce the product. My metal working experience was most useful, and I was soon building complex tools for the welding process in our workshop. Lew was very kind and accepting of me, even when he did not agree with my suggestions. We learned to discuss matters as engineers, arguing about our ideas logically and respectfully. For lunch, the whole family would gather in Father's office, where Mom brought the food. It was a wonderful example of teamwork. Everyone knew what was going on in every aspect of the business. Esme's mother was on the leather production floor the entire day, never taking a rest. She had an eagle eye and noticed everything, even before something went wrong. Esme's father was an expert in leather and would decide how to best utilize each piece. It was a very competitive business, and efficient cutting of the leather was essential. Norman became a skillful buyer of materials and supplies. It was a pleasure to work together as a family. I grew up as an only child, so being in a family with several siblings was a new and pleasant experience for me.

We began to look for other products to manufacture in the plastics area. The machines were versatile, and we used our creativity to produce our own tools to manufacture any new product that came to mind. I loved the freedom to generate ideas and test them in the market. I felt at home in the family and full of enthusiasm for developing new products.

One product we started manufacturing became the key to our future success — ring binders. In those days, vinyl ring binders were the cheap end of the business. They were poorly made and did not last long, like the leather or sewn binders did. We began to improve the product, step by step, and we also developed several ways to decorate them. One process, developed by Lew, was the appliqué print — letters were welded onto the surface of the binder, giving it a raised, three-dimensional effect. This was a very attractive but complicated process and became the door-opener for our sales because no one else knew how to do it. Our ring binders were beautiful and sturdy, and Weldo Plastics became the leading company in this industry in South Africa. Our main customers were manufacturers who required catalogs for their products.

We had an almost exclusive product, but it required a sales presentation each time. I began to go out and deal with top executives in companies, showing them all the unique features and helping design the binders. I began to bring in large orders for thousands of binders. My father-in-law, who was experienced at selling his products, remarked to me that I was a good salesman. I was surprised to hear this — I had a poor opinion of salesmen and did not like to be called one. I denied that I was a salesman and explained that I just made sure the customer ordered a suitable product, because I knew the product so well. He replied, "That is what a good salesman has to do!"

In time, I came to accept that I really was a good salesman. I used to tell customers when they were making a mistake, arguing against ideas that would have resulted in poor products. I totally rejected the view that "the customer is always right," because often the customer is ignorant! One customer begun to call me "Molotov" after the Soviet foreign minister who always said no to every proposal put to him. Despite that, this customer used to give me large orders and sent me other customers. I enjoyed myself, and walking out with several large orders in one day gave me satisfaction and confidence. We never hired another salesman — we were all selling when needed, and we were receiving enough orders to keep us happy.

Our plastics company began to be very profitable. We produced results that were impossible in the leather industry. But there was one major issue — the political situation in our country. I was feeling more certain than ever that this apartheid regime was going to end in a bloodbath, that one cannot and should not keep a whole population forever oppressed. The feeling I had while at university that I did not plan to live in Africa for the rest of my life came back to me. Esme and I had three young children by then — Ruven, born in February 1959; Julia, born in November 1960; and Avril, born in September 1962 — and I worried about their futures. I didn't want them to grow up with the racial attitude of the white population. Our son, at the age of three, was dominating our "garden boy" — a man of thirty — by instructing him to place him in the wheelbarrow and walk around the property. The gardener complied. He called Ruven "the little boss."

I began to speak to the family about emigration. They shared my discomfort with the situation. Slowly, we all began to think of emigrating. Then we made a long-term plan. Lew went to the United States and Canada, met some people and inquired about our potential as immigrants. He chose Toronto. The South African government had tough rules about taking out money abroad, so emigrating required a complex, step-by-step plan to get out.

Then, suddenly, Esme's father became very ill with cancer and died. We were all devastated. Her mother and Norman were running the leather factory, Lew was working to establish a small plastics factory in Toronto and I was running the plastics company in

Johannesburg. We started to reduce the leather factory's production, planning to close it down, and I managed to sell the plastics factory successfully. Now we could all move to Toronto.

Esme and I arrived in Toronto in 1964, but it took three years before we were all able to gather there. It was a large migration: Lew and Sonia with three children, Norman, Esme and I with our three children and my parents and Esme's mother, a total of fourteen people. We all threw ourselves into work with the small company, which was still named Weldo Plastics Ltd.

When Esme and I arrived in Toronto we decided that we needed to integrate into the community. First, we joined Temple Emanu-El, a Reform synagogue. We became active in the life of the synagogue; Esme took on a voluntary teaching job and I served on the board and at one time served as president. Later we found the ORT organization in Toronto. After I gave a talk about the two occasions in my life when ORT had served me so well, I was immediately invited to work with them, as was Esme. In time, we developed a close relationship with many friends there. Esme served as president of the Toronto women's ORT and I as president of the Toronto men's ORT. We served for many years, and Esme brought in many new members who later served as presidents and volunteers.

Through ORT I became involved in Miles for Millions, an umbrella fundraising organization for many volunteer organizations in Toronto. All faiths and charitable organizations were partners. I was on the board, and I learned much from the chairman, an important official of Shell Canada. It is an art to conduct a meeting with many members, some of whom do not like each other. I served on this board for many years as a representative for ORT. We had thousands of kids and adults walking thirty-two kilometres as a fundraiser for ORT. It was a great responsibility — things could go wrong, and did, but we raised millions of dollars every year.

Around this time there was an established group of Holocaust survivors that was meeting, and I joined them. We were meeting in the Jewish Federation building and by the early 1980s there was a move to build a Holocaust Memorial Centre. Many years went by before this could be achieved. I met with Nate Leipciger at Temple Emanu-El, and we became friends. He too was a Holocaust survivor and went through the camps with his father, as I did. We both began to speak about our experiences at gatherings. Later we began to speak at schools. I served for many years on the board of the Holocaust Memorial Centre in Toronto after it was built in 1986 and made friends with many survivors.

After four years of challenging work and a good deal of worry, our company became profitable. We were all selling, the three of us, even while doing our management duties, product design jobs, purchasing jobs, machine design duties, fiscal management and machine purchasing. My special job was training and supervising the sales force. My father took on the warehouse supervision in our factory. He was a skillful record keeper — our auditors assured us that there was never an error in the warehouse. He did all his record-keeping on paper and cards. Later, when we installed a computer program, there were big errors! Esme's mother hadn't waited long before coming to work at the factory. Since she had been working in a factory from the day she was married, she quickly established herself in the finishing and packing department and took over the management of the department. My mother-in-law was in the factory from opening, at 8:00 a.m., till closing time. She lived in an apartment quite far from the factory but refused to take any transport but the bus. We begged and argued, offering to have a driver pick her up, but we could not win her over. Hilda worked with several young women in the factory, and they respected her skill and strength. Sometimes there were funny exchanges between a new worker and Mrs. Cohen — she would show them how to lift a carton onto the pallet, alone, while they called for help.

I worked in one room with my brothers-in-law, Lew and Norman. That way, we all knew what was going on and could stand in for each other. We focused on ring binders as a mainstay of the business. I put much of my energy into sales, developing a process that I insisted all our salespeople follow. We moved several times, each time to larger premises. Then we obtained the North American rights to a different type of ring fitting — the Slanted D ring. It represented a major advantage over the usual round rings because it could hold 30 per cent more paper and the pages lay flat, not shifting and needing to be re-positioned when the binder was opened, but these points had to be clearly explained to the purchaser. The D ring's features gave us a tremendous advantage in the marketplace.

We expanded our sales to Montreal and hired Ike Banoun, a young, Jewish salesman from Cairo, Egypt. In time he became our best salesman and he remained a friend of mine for life, long after he left our company and established himself in Los Angeles.

When we decided it was time to start selling in the United States, we couldn't afford a large advertising budget, so I began to offer a free talk to companies that were giving courses about writing manuals. All manuals require a binder! I developed a talk for about one hour on how to design a good binder and travelled wherever the talk could be given. After my talk, I would distribute our literature and then chat with the participants over a beer. When I returned home, there were always calls waiting for me. Sales began to rise in the United States. Eventually we purchased a bankrupt bindery in Chicago and within a few years that Chicago company (Durand Manufacturing) exceeded our Canadian sales. We transferred all our technical and sales techniques to Chicago and were soon supplying the largest American companies, like all the auto manufacturers in Detroit, with manual binders and catalogue binders. We had a full art department to design gorgeous binders, and our appliqué technique was shining.

We won the gold, silver and bronze prizes in every competition in our industry. During an election in Canada, all three parties ordered the election manuals from us. They were not very happy when they saw all three binders displayed side by side with the slogan "All three parties agree…."

In 1968, on a visit to Germany to see a manufacturing supplier of ring fittings, I had an interesting experience that had a bearing on my war years. When I arrived at the airport, I was greeted by a company representative who said that he would be my translator, since the company staff did not speak English. I assured him that I did not require his services, that I spoke German quite well. He was surprised and asked me where I had learned German, and I replied, "In Dachau." That wasn't true — I knew German from Lithuania, but it was my way to remind them about their Nazi past.

The following morning, I spent most of the day in their factory boardroom, talking to the president and engineers about products and orders. No one said a word about my history, but after the meeting the vice-president of finance came up to me, pulled me aside and asked me if I was a Jew. "Yes, I am," I said. "And you were in Dachau?" Yes, again. "Come," he said, "let us go and have a chat somewhere over coffee." I immediately sensed that he wanted to tell me that he had been a Nazi, yet I went along with him to a coffee house. When we sat down he started by telling me that he joined the Nazi Party when he was eighteen years old. I was not planning to have an argument with him. I just said, "I suppose you had to join." "No," he said, "I *wanted* to join." Then he proceeded to tell me that his father, who had been a diplomat in the Weimar Republic, before Hitler, warned him not to join "these bad people," and he had walked away from his father, furious. When his father repeated the advice, he turned to his father and told him that if he said it a third time, he would report him to the Gestapo; he added, with amazement in his voice, "I was prepared to send my father to Dachau!"

I was taken aback by this statement. It's one thing to disagree about politics, but to send your father to a concentration camp to die? So, I carefully asked him if his father was a bad father to him. "He was a wonderful father!" he exclaimed. Then he told me how, when he heard "that man" (Hitler) speak, he felt a cold chill running down his spine, that he was ready to do "anything" for him.

When I heard him say "anything," I thought he must have been in the SS, and if so, I was out of there! I would not have spoken another word to him. I carefully asked him if he had done "anything." He understood immediately where I was going with this question. "No," he responded, "I did not do the pig-work [*Schweinerei* in German]. I was a soldier, wounded in the Battle of Stalingrad [the largest battle of the war]." I was relieved. Then I asked him, "Did you know what the Nazis did in your name?" He replied, "Yes, I saw it. I was present when they gathered a number of peasants in the Ukraine, pushed them into a wooden church, poured gasoline on it and burned them to death."

I commented that it appeared that Germans were now saying that they did not know that such atrocities were committed. (Remember, this was 1968 — now Germany is fully cognizant of its history.) "Don't you understand," he said, "we are so totally ashamed? We have committed crimes that will not be forgiven for one thousand years!" That comment brought a smile to my face — Hitler used to say in his speeches that he was building a state for the future, that in one thousand years' time people would still talk about this, their greatest hour. Now my new friend was telling me about one thousand years of shame. And then he added something that I have never forgotten. He said, "I want you to understand that I joined the Nazi Party not because I wanted to be a murderer, but because I was an idealist! I was ready to give my life for my country!"

I learned a good deal from this conversation. It gave me insight into the potential for young people to follow a leader blindly, even to total ruin.

~

In 1971, I fulfilled the old dream I had as a thirteen-year-old — I purchased a small plane, a single-engine Piper Comanche 250 HP, and became a pilot. I had restarted my flying education in 1968, taking lessons and earning my first license in 1969, after thirty-four hours of instruction. I purchased my plane from Skycharter and stored it at their hangar at Pearson International Airport. Our good friend Irving Shoichet owned the company. We are still especially close friends with his wife, Dorothy Shoichet, an art collector, and their children. Sadly, Irving died some years ago, in 2008.

I soon discovered that fog or clouds often stopped me from flying to Chicago or New York. I also had a scary experience in the summer of 1974, when I took my family flying to Nova Scotia and Prince Edward Island. On the way back, we stopped at Moncton to refuel. The clouds were low, but I thought I would be able to stay at three thousand feet, under the clouds. I didn't have an Instrument Rating (which would qualify me to fly in clouds) at the time, and in order to fly I had to see the horizon at all times. We took off, and within a few minutes, I was totally inside the clouds and could not see anything! I knew how dangerous this was. It takes only a few minutes for a pilot to lose control of an aircraft. Luckily, I had been trying to teach myself to observe the instruments while flying, foreseeing just such an event. I told myself that my test was now — if I panicked, we were lost. I carefully kept the plane level and called the Moncton tower, saying I was in "instrument weather," but not qualified, and to please get me back to the airport. The controller gave me a vector (an angle of direction to fly), told me to "keep her level" and to turn around slowly. I did just that. After a while he instructed me to start a slow descent. Soon I was out of the clouds and the runway was right in front of me. I was so relieved to have landed safely, but my shirt was wet with sweat. There and then I decided to seek instrument qualification, but I was happy to know that I do not panic in moments of distress.

In 1975, I earned my Instrument Rating, which allowed me to fly in clouds and at night. Now I was a real pilot! I flew my family to Florida, and I flew regularly to the US and in Canada on business trips. I absolutely loved it! After flying a total of four hundred hours, I sold the plane and took up soaring. Flying a glider is sheer poetry of flight.

~

My work hours were long, and it fell on Esme to deal with the children during the day. I also asked Esme to come with me to exhibitions where we were showing our wares. Esme was a great salesperson, and her charm and smarts got us many customers from the shows. When she was away from home, my mother and father, who lived with us, looked after the children.

The weekends were my time to be with Esme and our children, Ruven, Julia and Avril. Every Friday afternoon when I got home, Esme had already packed up the wagon and the tent-trailer, and we left immediately for a camping trip. We visited every camping park in Ontario, I think! During the summer, for a two-week vacation, we travelled further. We flew on a commercial airline to Calgary then drove to Vancouver. I flew the family to Florida and to Nova Scotia. We went camping to Kapuskasing and on to Moosonee and many more places in Canada and the United States. Our kids saw a good deal of our country. I was so happy to travel across this wonderful land with my family.

My father worked until he was over eighty, then he became ill and died at age eighty-four. My mother lived with us almost until the end of her life, when we had to place her in a nursing home, where she did not live long. She had lived to see three grandchildren and four great-grandchildren. She was full of life in her old age, though at the end she hated her frailty and dependence, and she did not wish to continue in that state. She died on August 12, 1994, at age ninety-two.

Esme's mother worked at the factory until she was over eighty, when a sudden internal bleed forced her to go to the hospital nearby. When we arrived at the hospital, the nurse told us that this lady was a bit confused because she was talking about coming from work at a factory. We assured the nurse it was so! I always had a good relationship with Hilda. She died at age ninety-two.

In the late 1970s, we began to receive offers for our companies, in Canada and in the United States. Eventually, in 1981, feeling like we were ready to do something else, it was time to sell. After prolonged negotiations, we sold to Jostens, an American conglomerate, which was later bought out by Newell, an even bigger corporation.

I soon had an idea for another business. It was still 1981, and this was the time of the minicomputer. I hired a good friend, Norman Dash, a skilled computer programmer, and we designed a program for small businesses so that they would need only a telephone line and a screen with a keyboard and a printer to have access to a computer. We would give them access to a smart program for all their business needs, from inventory to payroll, for a small monthly fee. When we were ready to begin selling the program, the microcomputer by IBM arrived on the market. We were out of business! Now everyone could afford a small computer. So, in 1982, I closed the business.

I was not sitting idle for long — an offer came to take on the management of a large company with three factories producing injection moulded food containers, like the kind that hold sour cream. The company had lost millions in the previous five years. Could I fix it? I took on the job. I was searching for something I could improve to allow us to charge more for our product in a very competitive market. I had to learn how the company operated. I instituted new rules about cleanliness, and I fixed certain things, but then I found the key: the quality of the text and images on the containers was very poor. However, all our competitors' printing was equally terrible. I focused on the issue and uncovered the simple reason — our long-time employees had never learned how the machine was to be set up! We solved the problem and began to print perfectly. I checked in the US market — the same problem. I rushed into the US market, appointed seven agents and began selling at far better prices. Suddenly we were showing a profit! The owners of the company were pleased and then quickly sold the company.

I ran a few other businesses when, in 1985, Esme decided to start a private vocational school for people who had dropped out of school or just wanted to learn a job skill. Six years earlier, in 1979, Esme had decided to create a special school for teenagers with learning problems when our youngest daughter, Avril, had some problems learning and we could not find a suitable school. Esme had named it Spring-field School for Girls. It achieved its aims by applying innovative ways of learning. Esme argued that even if a student had trouble with the multiplication table, they needed to know how to manage a bank account, and they needed to know basic things like who Shakespeare was, who the prime minister of Canada was, how to use a computer and so on. The students all did very well.

Then, Esme joined the Toronto School of Business franchise and opened a school in Oshawa. She later added another campus in Pickering and a third one in Cobourg. It was a very fine school, with hundreds of students, and Esme ran the school for fifteen years. One day, Esme invited me to join her in the school. I was to develop a program to help the students find jobs after completing their studies. Since I had hired many people in my business career, I knew what to do. I developed a course where we taught them how to find a job by some unusual tactics. I urged the students not to seek work in the usual places, like newspaper ads or notice boards (this was before the internet), since the competition was too great, and not to send uninvited applications to companies. Instead, they were to find a few companies close to home and then research the details of these companies. Then they were to visit the companies at 5:00 p.m., go to the parking lot and ask the exiting employees to give them the name and telephone number of the manager of the department where they wanted to work. After approaching that specific person, they were to display their knowledge of the company and how they could contribute to its success. That method worked very well. We also taught them how to interview successfully, showing them confident gestures to use. A video camera showed them how they conducted themselves during a mock interview and helped them eliminate mistakes in their behaviour. We were very successful, getting some 85 per cent of students employed within two weeks of completion of the course. I really enjoyed working with the students. Many were very unsure of themselves, and we were successful in building up their confidence.

Epilogue

In 1999, Esme and I participated in a group tour called From Anguish to Hope with thirty university students from Canada, accompanying them to Poland and Lithuania to visit the concentration camps. The organizer of this program, Eli Rubinstein, became a good friend. This journey grew into the program the March of Remembrance and Hope, founded in 2001, and I participated again in 2016 and in 2018 together with Esme.

In 1999, I invited my cousin Dalia, who still lives in Norway, to come to Lithuania with us. In Vilnius, the present capital of Lithuania, we met with Professor Dr. Vytautas Landsbergis, then speaker of the Lithuanian parliament and former head of state. This man was Dalia's "cousin" when she was with the Lithuanian family during the war. We were received very warmly by him at his home, and he told us many stories about Dalia as a little girl. He was very touched by her visit.

We also visited Kaunas and the area of the ghetto where Dalia and I had lived. At the Ninth Fort, I said to Dalia, "Here, on this path, your mother's parents, and your aunt with her husband and children, walked to their deaths." It was a sad and touching moment for all of us.

In about the year 2000, after retiring from the business world, I began to devote more time to the Holocaust Memorial Centre, now called the Sarah and Chaim Neuberger Holocaust Education Centre. Judy Cohen, a survivor and a fine speaker, was also active there. She suggested that we build a wall display of photos of our speakers' panel with a storyboard attached to each photo. There were many problems with the execution of the project, so I took it on and designed a structure for the images to slide on, with the story boards behind the images, saving room on the wall. When the display opened, it was greeted with appreciation. One executive from another organization asked me to build the same for him. I realized that I had another business here! I called it Tribute Displays and began offering photographic displays to schools and organizations. I found many customers and became quite busy producing and installing the displays. I did everything, including printing the pictures and installing the rails and the frames. Sometimes Esme came to help me install the displays. Some organizations kept me busy, changing the displays at regular intervals.

One project to which I devoted many hours over a few years was in saving the video recordings of Holocaust survivors by our Holocaust Centre. In 1987, Nate Leipciger, as chairperson of our centre, initiated video recording of our survivor members on used beta tapes. Then the tapes were packed away in cartons, with no clear plan of how to utilize them. In 2006, I asked for the tapes and had students help me clean them and sort them out. Someone donated bookshelves and I assigned each tape a label. I then managed to obtain some funding to copy all the tapes to DVD. I recruited Esme to do the transcriptions, which required much time and research. She worked very diligently and two years later we had over ten thousand pages of text! University students and researchers began asking for texts and DVDS on specific subjects; Esme was able to give them the materials they were seeking. We also made copies for family members, who were delighted to discover that their parents had left such a legacy. I then began videotaping survivors and added to the collection. Recently, the Shoah Foundation, with substantial sums granted from the Canadian federal government, has taken charge of the tapes and is digitizing them for the future. I was very happy to have helped save the tapes for future generations.

Over the years, Esme and I developed a group of close friends in Toronto. Dr. Esther Gelcer has been our dear friend since her arrival in Toronto many years ago from South Africa and Israel. Bernice Schwartz, a gifted artist, and her children and grandchildren are close friends. I came to value many friends who are survivors, like Pinchas Gutter and the late Bill Glied. We also greatly value the closeness we feel to Rabbi Arthur Bielfeld and Renée Sieburth, lifelong friends from Temple Emanu-El, where we enjoy many friendships. And I must also mention my relative and friend Colin Soskolne, professor emeritus from the University of Alberta who, in his retirement, continues to travel internationally to improve medical sciences. Esme and I are also close to Professor Robert Jan van Pelt and his wife, Miriam Greenbaum, who we met accidentally in a restaurant many years ago. Both are involved in research and commemoration of the Holocaust.

We enjoy being part of our children's lives. Ruven has a fine career with Avanade Inc., a major international computer consulting company. He lives in New York, where he serves as director of innovation for the eastern United States. His wife, Deborah, is an accomplished computer specialist and systems analyst. Our daughter Julia is a very successful psychotherapist in private practice. She is married to Nathan, a businessman and an artist. Our youngest daughter, Avril, lives with her husband, Martin, and their three children in Owen Sound, Ontario, and they are a very happy family. We love dearly and enjoy the company of our six grandchildren: Anita, Ilana and Ethan; and Sarah, Martin and Robin. And we are close to Esme's brother Norman, his wife, Violette, and their children, Philip and Andre, as well as to Rochelle and Babette, the children of Esme's late brother, Lew.

Over the years, I have visited many schools to speak about my experiences during the Holocaust. Like all survivors, I stress the lessons of the Holocaust: don't be prejudiced, avoid hate, understand the tragedy that befell the Jewish people. Now that I am retired, I have expanded my visits. In January 2012, the United Nations offices in South Africa, together with local Holocaust museums, invited me to speak about the Holocaust in Johannesburg, Durban and Cape Town. My dear cousin Zamie Liknaitzky, a lawyer, and his wife, Natalie, an art curator and dealer, arranged the speaking tour. Esme and I travelled to all three cities together, and it was particularly moving for me to speak at the university from which I had graduated. In 2016 I addressed over twelve thousand students in Canada. I made my own bookings and drove myself to the schools, and the teachers received me most kindly. Some letters I receive from students move me greatly. Not only do they appreciate the horror of the Holocaust, but my own resilience in surviving and fighting for my education gives them hope that they too can achieve something in life.

In July 2017 I decided to fulfill an aeronautical dream — jumping from an airplane. To mark the 150th anniversary of Canada, I wore a shirt with the slogan Canada 150. My family was not too thrilled about the project, but I know that now the parachutes land like gliders, so there is less likelihood of breaking a leg. When I called the company at the airport and they heard that I was eighty-nine years old, they wanted to look me over first. They accepted me and offered for me to jump without charge if they could invite the press. I agreed. The jump went well. In the first moment when we stepped out of the plane at 13,000 feet and tumbled head over heel, it felt like my heart stopped. I thought that I would fly like a bird — but I was actually falling like a rock! It was a great feeling though. When the parachute opened, I felt a strong jerk upwards as we stopped the 120-kilometre-per-hour fall and began the glide to earth. Some saw me on television and in the papers, so people I hadn't seen in years began calling me!

I am still in good health, swimming every day of the year, and I am always occupied with innovative ideas, inventing things and creating new products.

In March 2018 we celebrated my ninetieth birthday and our sixtieth wedding anniversary. I told the gathering of family and friends that to reach the sixtieth anniversary is a privilege, but to reach ninety is a surprise.

Esme is well, and we are so happy together, still in love.

Afterword: Messages to and from Students

Dear students,

When your school invites me to speak, I am given a one-hour time slot. I respect the needs of your teachers and your timetable, so I always keep one eye on the clock. When I see my time is running out, I must quickly decide which stories to tell and which ones to skip. In this book, I included events and experiences that are important to me. There will be some stories you recognize and some that will be new to you.

When you study European history, particularly World War II, you also touch on the Holocaust. You read about the millions of people who suffered and died. I am a survivor and a witness to those terrible events. I am now ninety years old. Soon there will be no more survivors and witnesses. I want you to understand what the tragedy of the Holocaust means to the Jewish people.

I feel an obligation to inspire young people to be aware, to be involved and to add their voices to advocate for justice. Talking about my experiences would not have been possible if I hadn't had your support and your feedback. Your personal letters, some excerpts of which follow this message, showed me that you found my stories memorable. Your interest kept me wanting to come back to meet the new Grade 10 and Grade 11 students, year after year.

I especially want to thank the wonderful teachers I have met over the years. Your dedication to your students and to this topic is heart-warming and impressive.

Elly Gotz

Today, you told us your life story at my school. I just thought I would let you know how much it touched me. My family is going through a rough time at the moment. We have events going on that make me really stressed out and sad. Sometimes, I like to think about what it would be like to end my life. Your story made me realize how foolish it would be…. You gave me hope. You accomplished so much despite your hardships and I thought I would just thank you for showing me it will get better. So, here it goes: Thank you. I know you have been through harder times than mine, but you give me hope and that's all I really need. — J

…there was something about your story that really hit a chord in me. To be honest, it has not left my mind since your presentation. The focus on forgiveness and not living life with hatred was so powerful coming from someone with so many reasons to hate. I wanted to let you know that you have inspired me. You have inspired me to utilize perspective and to realize that anger is just a sentence to a horrible life. You inspired me to forgive and to be brave. Your story helped further my knowledge of this genocide and brought insight to the horrors you lived. — Jennifer

Due to my age, and my time period, the war is not something I generally think about, or genocide for that matter. …however, hearing what you had to say today has opened my mind greatly, especially your words on genocide. I realize now how aware we as a society need to be on accepting people's ethnicities, religions and cultures. …Moving forward, I want to strive to be a more accepting person. — Michael

...the words that struck me the most were your last words to the Grade 10s at my school. You said, "There's a battle between two wolves inside us all. One is evil. One wolf of anger, jealousy, greed, resentment, inferiority, lies and ego. The other is good. It's joy, peace, love, hope, humility, kindness and truth. Which wolf will win the battle, the good or the bad? The wolf you feed." And Sir Elly Gotz, I vow to always feed the good wolf. Your speech really touched my heart. Thank you. — Michelle

Your story of how you overcame your adversities is amazing. I cannot believe how strong you are... I also love the way you were able to get over your hatred for the German nation after the Holocaust. I hope I will be able to achieve the same strength as you have one day. You have truly taught me that if you put your mind to something and want to achieve it you will. — Gavin

In history, we learn a lot about the facts and statistics about the wars, and it creates a feeling that it is all unbelievable. It is difficult to comprehend that such an awful series of events took place, and learning about it all, I question my faith in humanity. Your story brought everything we learned to life...It was a real privilege to have the opportunity to be taken through your life, and I thank you for being so kind to share your journey. ... Thank you for making me realize that there are so many things in life that I should be thankful for every day, and that I should start living life to the fullest. You have made a great impact on me. — Isabella

Glossary

Aktion (German; pl. *Aktionen*) The brutal roundup of Jews for forced labour, forcible resettlement into ghettos, mass murder by shooting or deportation to death camps.

Ältestenrat (German; Jewish Council of Elders) Also known as Judenrat, Jewish Council. A group of Jewish leaders appointed by the Germans to administer and provide services to the local Jewish population under occupation and enforce Nazi policies and demands. The chairman of the Ältestenrat in the Kovno ghetto, Dr. Elchanan Elkes (1879–1944) was a respected physician who was unanimously elected to the position by local Jewish leaders and supported Jewish resistance activities in the ghetto. Elkes was seen by ghetto inmates as a person of integrity even though he was forced to implement Nazi policies. The Kovno ghetto was dissolved in July 1944, and Dr. Elkes was sent to the Landsberg concentration camp, where he died in October 1944. *See also* Kovno ghetto.

antisemitism Prejudice, discrimination, persecution or hatred against Jewish people, institutions, culture and symbols.

apartheid (Afrikaans; apartness) The South African policy of racial segregation that favoured the country's white minority and discriminated against non-whites. The policy was implemented in 1948 and instituted laws that controlled property ownership, employment, sexual relationships, education and voting rights of non-white citizens. The legislation supporting apartheid was repealed in 1991, though its social and economic effects are ongoing.

Appellplatz (German; the place for roll call) The area in Nazi camps where inmates had to assemble to be counted. Roll calls were part of a series of daily humiliations for prisoners, who were often made to stand completely still for hours, regardless of the weather conditions.

Bruch, Max (1838–1920) The German Romantic composer who wrote *Kol Nidrei*, a celebrated composition for cello and orchestra that incorporates the traditional melody for *Kol Nidrei*, the prayer that opens the evening service at the start of Yom Kippur, the holiest day of the Jewish year. Bruch's music was banned by the Nazis because they assumed he was Jewish, though he was in fact Protestant.

Central Historical Commission (CHC) An agency of the Central Committee of Liberated Jews in the American Zone of Occupation created to collect documentation and publish research about the Holocaust. From 1945–1950, the CHC, whose headquarters were in Munich, opened about fifty branches in the various DP camps in Germany, where survivor testimonies were recorded and questionnaires distributed. The commission also supported endeavours in education, culture, religion, law, emigration and employment.

Dachau The Nazis' first concentration camp, which was established primarily to house political prisoners in March 1933. The Dachau camp was located about sixteen kilometres northwest of Munich in southern Germany. The number of Jews interned there rose considerably after Kristallnacht pogroms on the night of November 9–10, 1938. In 1942 a crematorium area was constructed next to the main camp. By the spring of 1945, Dachau and its subcamps held more than 67,665 registered prisoners — 43,350 categorized as political prisoners and 22,100 as Jews. As the American Allied forces neared the camp in April 1945, the Nazis forced 7,000 prisoners, primarily Jews, on a gruelling death march to Tegernsee, another camp in southern Germany.

DP (displaced persons) camps Facilities set up by the Allied authorities and the United Nations Relief and Rehabilitation Administration (UNRRA) in October 1945 to resolve the refugee crisis that arose at the end of World War II. The camps provided temporary shelter and assistance to the millions of people — not only Jews — who had been displaced from their home countries as a result of the war and helped them prepare for resettlement. *See also* United Nations Relief and Rehabilitation Administration (UNRRA).

Hofmekler, Michael (Misha) (1898–?) A well-known violinist from Vilna, Lithuania, who was decorated by the Lithuanian president in 1932 for his contribution to Lithuanian folk music. With the German occupation of Lithuania, Hofmekler was confined to the Kovno ghetto with the rest of the Jewish population, where he formed and conducted a ghetto orchestra. He was sent to Dachau and was liberated in late April 1945. After the war he conducted the X-Concentration Camp Orchestra in the St. Ottilien DP camp in Germany. *See also* Kovno ghetto; St. Ottilien.

Jablonskis, Jonas (1906–1941) A Lithuanian journalist who worked for ELTA, the Lithuanian news agency, and published the illegal "Free Lithuania" newspaper during World War II. Jablonskis was arrested and shot by the Soviets in June 1941.

Jäger Report A report written by Karl Jäger, commander of Einsatzkommando 3, a Nazi killing squad operating in Latvia, Lithuania and Belarus. Written on December 1, 1941, the nine-page report documents the murders of 137,346 people, mostly Jews, from July 2, 1941, to November 25, 1941, listing the date and place of the murders, as well as the categories of those murdered — such as Jews, communists, the mentally ill. The report declared that the Einsatzkommando had solved "the Jewish problem" in Lithuania, leaving only 34,500 "working Jews" alive.

Kadish, George (1910–1977; born Zvi [Hirsh] Kadushin) A Jewish photographer who secretly documented everyday life in the Kovno ghetto using home-made cameras. Kadish's numerous photographs are a significant contribution to the documentation of ghetto life during the Holocaust. *See also* Kovno ghetto.

Kaufering A subcamp of the Dachau concentration camp in southern Germany established in June 1944. There were eleven camps in the Kaufering camp system, housing 30,000 inmates who provided the labour to build underground aircraft factories that would be safe from Allied bombs. The prisoners, the majority of whom were Jews from Hungary and Lithuania, slept in partially submerged earthen huts and suffered from malnutrition, disease and brutal working conditions. As the US army approached in April 1945, the Nazis forced the inmates to march toward Dachau, where some stayed and were liberated on April 28, 1945; others were forced to continue on a death march, and the survivors were liberated in May 1945. In the ten months that Kaufering existed, approximately half its inmates died.

Kinderaktion (German; children's action) The SS-coordinated roundup and murder of children in the ghettos and concentration camps. Children were singled out in part because they required food but were too young to be effective workers. In the Kovno ghetto, a *Kinderaktion* took place on March 27–28, 1944, when German soldiers rounded up approximately one thousand children along with elderly and sick people and placed them in trucks and buses playing loud music to muffle the screams of the children and their parents. Some accounts state that the children were murdered at the Ninth Fort that day; other accounts state that they were sent to be gassed in Auschwitz.

Kovno ghetto A restricted area for Jews in the suburb of Slobodka, in Kaunus, or Kovno, Lithuania, established on August 15, 1941. It was initially divided into two sections, the "small" and "large" ghettos, but the small ghetto was liquidated in October 1941. The

Jewish population — approximately 30,000 people — was contained in an area that had previously housed 8,000 people. In the months after the ghetto was established, the Nazis carried out a number of *Aktionen,* and by the end of October, only 18,000 Jews remained in the ghetto. A Jewish Council oversaw the administration of the ghetto and had to meet a daily quota for forced labour; they also initiated educational and cultural activities. The ghetto was officially turned into a concentration camp on September 15, 1943, and was liquidated on July 12, 1944, with the remaining Jews taken in cattle cars to Stuthoff and Dachau concentration camps. The ghetto was then burned to the ground, killing almost all of those who were still hiding there. It is estimated that only 2,000 Jews from Kovno survived the war. *See also Aktion*; Ältestenrat; Dachau; *Kinderaktion*; Ninth Fort; Stutthof.

March of Remembrance and Hope (MRH) An annual ten-day educational program that connects post-secondary students with Holocaust survivors and educators. The MRH, founded in 2001, brings Canadian students of diverse ethnic and faith backgrounds to Germany and Poland to commemorate victims, recognize survivors and rescuers, and create an atmosphere of communal learning and hope.

Molotov-Ribbentrop pact *See* Treaty of Non-Aggression between Germany and the USSR.

Ninth Fort A Nazi killing site near Kaunus, Lithuania, where an estimated 50,000 people, mostly Jews, including groups transported from other countries, were murdered and disposed of in mass graves.

Oleiski, Jacob (1901–1981) The director of the ORT Jewish trade school in Kaunus before World War II and then director of Fachschule, the vocational school in the Kovno ghetto. Oleiski was deported to Dachau in 1944, and after the war he established ORT schools in the DP camps in the American Zone of Germany. He immigrated to Israel in 1949 and became director general of ORT

Israel, establishing a network of ORT schools there. *See also* Kovno ghetto; ORT.

Organization for Rehabilitation through Training (ORT) A vocational school system founded for Jews by Jews in Russia in 1880 to promote economic self-sufficiency in impoverished communities. The name ORT derives from the acronym of the Russian organization Obshestvo Remeslenogo Zemledelcheskogo Truda, Society for Trades and Agricultural Labour. ORT schools continued to operate through World War II, including in the Kovno and Warsaw ghettos. After the war, ORT set up rehabilitation programs for the survivors, serving approximately 85,000 people in 78 DP camps in Germany. Today, ORT is a non-profit organization that provides educational services to communities all over the world. *See also* Oleiski, Jacob.

Palanga (in Yiddish, Polangen) A Lithuanian resort town on the shores of the Baltic Sea with a population of about 700 Jews in 1940. The Jews of Palanga were involved in Zionist organizations, and many held leadership positions in the city. The Germans invaded Palanga on June 22, 1941, the first day of their attack on the Soviet forces. With the help of Lithuanian Nazi collaborators, all the Jews of Palanga were arrested a few days later and detained in the synagogue. Over 100 Jewish men were then taken to dig their own graves and were shot into them. The women and children were detained a while longer and then taken to a nearby forest and shot. Hundreds of Jewish children who had come to Palanga for summer camp were murdered as well. In 1991 a memorial in Hebrew, Yiddish and Lithuanian was erected to commemorate the brutal murders.

Provisional Government of Lithuania The temporary government set up by the Lithuanian Activist Front (LAF), a group of nationalist rebels who took up arms against the Soviet occupiers and proclaimed Lithuanian independence on June 23, 1941, a day after Germany invaded. The provisional government allied itself with the Nazis and passed numerous laws depriving Jews of their rights, inciting violence and horrific murders. The Germans disbanded the provisional government after six weeks of its rule.

Rauca, Helmut A Nazi SS master sergeant and the senior Nazi official in Kaunas, Lithuania. Rauca was responsible for the murder of over 10,000 Jews from the Kovno ghetto between 1941 and 1943, often picking which Jews would be executed and carrying out the murders himself. In 1982 he was discovered to be living in Toronto, Canada, and became the first Canadian to be charged with war crimes. Rauca was extradited to Germany, where he died in 1983 while awaiting trial.

Red Cross A humanitarian organization founded in 1863 to protect the victims of war. During World War II, the Red Cross provided assistance to prisoners of war by distributing food parcels and monitoring the situation in POW camps, and also provided medical attention to wounded soldiers and civilians, but did not intervene in how Jews were being treated by the Nazis. Much criticism has been levelled at the Red Cross for their inaction during the war, and the organization has admitted some of its shortcomings. Today, in addition to the international body, the International Committee of the Red Cross (ICRC), there are national Red Cross and Red Crescent societies in almost every country in the world.

Righteous Among the Nations A title bestowed by Yad Vashem, the Holocaust Martyrs' and Heroes' Remembrance Authority in Jerusalem, to honour non-Jews who risked their lives to help save Jews during the Holocaust. A commission was established in 1963 to award the title. If a person fits certain criteria and the story is carefully corroborated, the honouree is awarded with a medal and certificate and commemorated on the Wall of Honour at the Garden of the Righteous in Jerusalem.

Russian Revolution The 1917 February and October revolutions that led to the dissolution of the autocratic tsarist regime and the creation of a Communist government, respectively. The provisional government established after the February revolt was defeated by the Bolsheviks in October. The Bolshevik government – also referred to as the "reds" – was subsequently challenged by the "whites" or anti-Bolsheviks, which resulted in a five-year civil war.

St. Ottilien A DP camp, Jewish hospital and rehabilitation centre that was in a former Benedictine monastery near Munich, Germany. Approximately 5,000 concentration camp survivors were cared for in St. Ottilien from 1945–1948. The camp housed a school and an orchestra, and a police force kept the peace between the Jews, Germans and monks who lived in the complex. There is a small Jewish cemetery on the grounds of the monastery. *See also* DP camps; Hofmekler, Michael.

Stutthof A concentration camp established on September 2, 1939, near Danzig (Gdańsk), Poland. Initially its inmates were predominantly Poles, though the camp population also included Jews, political prisoners, criminals and others. In late summer of 1944, tens of thousands of Jews arrived from the ghettos in the Baltic States and Poland, as well as from Hungary via Auschwitz, and the population of the camp became predominantly Jewish. Altogether, Stutthof held around 110,000 prisoners, of which at least 65,000 died, mostly from overwork, disease, malnutrition, abuse and, especially toward the end of the war, lethal injection or gas. On January 25, 1945, 11,000 of the 50,000 camp inmates were forced on a death march. The survivors of the march were interred in a temporary camp and were liberated at the beginning of March 1945. Many of the inmates who remained behind in Stutthof died from hunger or typhus, or as a result of further evacuations and mass executions. The 100 inmates who remained hiding at Stutthof were liberated by Soviet forces on May 9, 1945.

Treaty of Non-Aggression between Germany and the USSR The treaty that was signed on August 24, 1939, and was colloquially known as the Molotov-Ribbentrop pact, after signatories Soviet foreign minister Vyacheslav Molotov and German foreign minister Joachim von Ribbentrop. The main provisions of the pact stipulated that the two countries would not go to war with each other and that they would both remain neutral if either one was attacked by a third party. One of the key components of the treaty was the division of various independent countries – including Poland – into Nazi and Soviet spheres of influence and areas of occupation. The Nazis breached the pact by launching a major offensive against the Soviet Union on June 22, 1941.

UNRRA An international relief agency created at a 44-nation conference in Washington, DC, on November 9, 1943, to provide economic assistance and basic necessities to war refugees. It was especially active in repatriating and assisting refugees in the formerly Nazi-occupied European nations immediately after World War II.

White Armbanders Supporters of the nationalist Lithuanian Activist Front (LAF), which was active in expelling the Soviets and welcoming the Germans in 1941, known for their white armbands and the violent and cruel pogroms they carried out against local Jews. *See also* Provisional Government of Lithuania.

Yiddish A language derived from Middle High German with elements of Hebrew, Aramaic, Romance and Slavic languages, and written in Hebrew characters. Spoken by Jews in east-central Europe for roughly a thousand years from the tenth century to the mid-twentieth century, it was still the most common language among European Jews until the outbreak of World War II. There are similarities between Yiddish and contemporary German.

Young Pioneers The Young Pioneer Organization of the Soviet Union, also called the Lenin All-Union Pioneer Organization, was a mass youth organization that instilled communist ideology in Soviet children ages ten to fifteen.

Photographs

1 Elly's father, Julius (Judel) Gotz. Kaunas, Lithuania, 1926.
2 Elly's mother, Sonja (née Wilentschuk) Gotz. Kaunas, Lithuania, 1926.
3 Joshua Gotz, Elly's paternal grandfather. Kaunas, Lithuania, 1934.
4 Bluma Gotz, Elly's paternal grandmother. Kaunas, Lithuania, 1934.

1

2

3

1 Elly, age six, on his first bicycle. Kaunas, Lithuania, 1934.
2 Elly riding his bike on the main street of Laisvės Alėja, the street on which his family lived. Kaunas, Lithuania, circa 1935.
3 Elly, age eight, on summer vacation in Kulautuva, Lithuania. 1936.

1 Elly with family. From left to right: Sonia, a relative; Elly's mother, Sonja; his uncle Samuel Gotz; his grandmother Bluma Gotz; Elly; his father, Julius; his grandmother Chaya Leah (Alte); and his grandfather Joshua Gotz. Kaunas, Lithuania, 1936.

2 Elly and his mother. Kaunas, Lithuania, 1937.

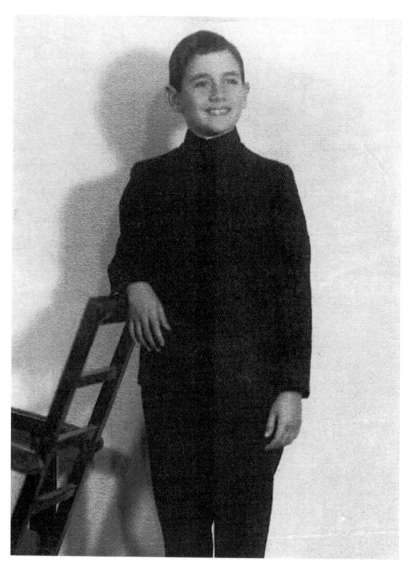

Elly at age thirteen in the uniform he was supposed to wear to high school, which he never got to attend due to Germany's invasion of Lithuania. Kaunas, Lithuania, 1941.

1

2

1   Elly (standing) teaching students in the ghetto Fachschule (trade school) in Kaunas. On Elly's right is Itzchak Kopilowitz, whom he reunited with in Tel Aviv in 2007. The photographer, George Kadish, captured this and many other images clandestinely in the ghetto in 1944; fifty years later, in 1994, Elly discovered the photo by coincidence at the United States Holocaust Memorial Museum in Washington, DC.

2   Reunion of students from the Kovno ghetto Fachschule. Clockwise from left: Elly Gotz; Itzchak Kopilowitz; Shmuel Elchanan; and Elly's cousin Chone Knebel. Not pictured, but at the reunion, was Dr. Shalom Eilati. Tel Aviv, 2007.

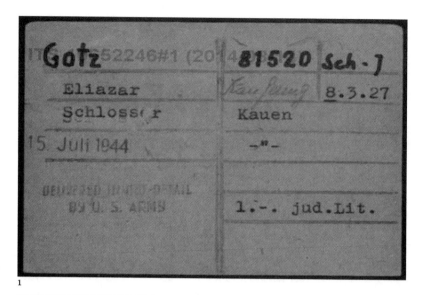

1 Elly's prisoner card from Kaufering, showing his age as one year older than he was, with his profession listed as *Schlosser*, locksmith. Kaufering, 1944. Photo credit: International Tracing Service (ITS) Bad Arolsen.

2 The Kaufering IV concentration camp as seen on April 29, 1945. These barracks are similar to the ones Elly Gotz lived in during his time in the Kaufering I subcamp of Dachau. Photo credit: United States Holocaust Memorial Museum, courtesy of National Archives and Records Administration, College Park.

1

2

1 Two of three concrete pumping plants on the west side of Weingut II, photo-
graphed by the deputy site manager in the spring of 1945. The building on the
right is where Elly worked, and the pipe from the pump he was stationed at can
be seen at far right, emerging from the building. Photo credit: Archive Manfred
Deiler, European Holocaust Memorial Foundation, Landsberg am Lech.

2 Construction site of the bomb-proof bunker with the code name "Weingut II."
Landsberg am Lech, 1945. Photo credit: Archive Manfred Deiler, European Holocaust Memorial Foundation, Landsberg am Lech.

1 Elly's cousin Dalia (centre) on the lap of her adoptive mother, Jadvyga Jablonskienė. On Jadvyga's left is her mother, Marija Žakevičienė. Kaunas, Lithuania, circa 1943.

2 Dalia reunited with her parents, David and Mary Wilentschuk, after the war. Geltendorf, Germany, 1946.

1 Elly and his mother, Sonja, after their emigration from Germany. Halden, Norway, 1947.

2 Elly's parents, Julius and Sonja, in Bulawayo, Rhodesia (now Zimbabwe), in the early 1950s.

3 Elly with a dead crocodile after hunting on the Zambezi River. Rhodesia (Zimbabwe), 1954.

1 Elly's graduation as an engineer from Witwatersrand University. Johannesburg,
   South Africa, 1952.
2 Elly on the day of his wedding. Johannesburg, South Africa, March 16, 1958.
3 Esme and Elly on their wedding day. Johannesburg, South Africa, March 16, 1958.
4 On their honeymoon by the Trevi Fountain. Rome, Italy, 1958.

1

2

1   Esme and Elly celebrating their wedding with their parents. From left to right: Esme's father, Abram; her mother, Hilda; Esme; Elly; his mother, Sonja; and his father, Julius. Johannesburg, South Africa, March 16, 1958.

2   Visiting family in Norway after their wedding. From left to right: Uncle Anatol (Tanchum); Elly; Uncle David; Cousin Dalia; Esme; Uncle Gedalie; Cousin Liv; Aunt Nata; Uncle Gedalie's sister-in-law; Uncle Gedalie's wife, Beks; and Aunt Mary. Oslo, Norway, 1958.

1 The Knebel family, Elly's cousins, after the war. From left to right: Nechama, Chone and Eta — who survived the Nazi camps — and Pesach, who survived in the Soviet Union. Their brother Ruven and their father Zalman died in Dachau. Kovno, Lithuania, 1968.

2 Elly's uncle Samuel Gotz and his aunt Ann on a visit to New York, circa 1980.

1

2

1   Elly (right) with Jacob Oleiski, the director of the Kaunas Ghetto Fachschule, who, after the war, was the director of the ORT schools in displaced persons camps in the American Zone in Germany. Elly and Dr. Oleiski reunited at an ORT conference in Montreal in 1968.

2   Elly (far right) with Esme (far left) receiving then-Governor General of Canada Roland Michener (second from the left) and his wife, Norah, on ORT day, when Esme and Elly both served as presidents of the organization. Toronto, 1971.

1 Elly with family at home in Toronto. From left to right: Elly's son, Ruven; Elly's
mother, Sonja; his wife, Esme; his daughter Avril; Elly; his father, Julius; and his
daughter Julia. 1970.

2 Elly with Esme's family. From left to right: Elly; Esme; Esme's mother, Hilda;
Norman's wife, Violette; Esme's brother Norman; Lew's wife, Sonia; and Esme's
brother Lew. Toronto, 1971.

Esme and Elly, Toronto, 1971.

1 Esme and Elly with their son, Ruven, on the occasion of his graduation from the University of Toronto in 1984.
2 Esme with daughters Avril (left) and Julia (right). Toronto, 1990.

1 Esme and Elly with their twin granddaughters, Ilana (left) and Anita (right) Gotz. Toronto, 1991.

2 Anita (left) and Ilana (right) at their graduation from university. Kingston, 2014.

3 The family of Elly's daughter Avril Kurr. In back, left to right: Elly's granddaughter Sarah; his daughter Avril; and his son-in-law Martin. In front: Elly's grandson Martin and his granddaughter Robin. Owen Sound, 2008.

4 Elly's grandson Ethan Gotz. Toronto, 2010.

1   Elly's son, Ruven Gotz, and Elly's daughter-in-law, Deborah Gotz. 2018.
2   Elly and his cousin Dalia. Spain, 2017.
3   Elly's cousin Liv and her husband, Harald. Oslo, Norway, 2018.
4   Elly with the granddaughters of his cousin Liv — Eva (left) and Ellie (right), who was named in Elly's honour. Oslo, Norway, 2018.

1

2

3

1 & 2 Elly with students on the March of Remembrance and Hope. In photo 1, far
right, is Elly's good friend Gary Schwartz of Toronto, who joined the group for a
few days. Poland, 2016. Photo credit: Laina Brown.

3 Elly speaking about his survival during the Holocaust to students at Sherwood
Secondary School. Hamilton, 2013.

Elly, age eighty-nine, as he jumps from an airplane. Cookstown, 2017.

Elly and Esme celebrating their sixtieth anniversary and Elly's ninetieth birthday. Toronto, March 2018.

Index

The Azrieli Foundation was established in 1989 to realize and extend the philanthropic vision of David J. Azrieli, C.M., C.Q., M.Arch. The Foundation's mission is to support a wide spectrum of initiatives in education and research. The Azrieli Foundation is an active supporter of programs in the fields of education, the education of architects, scientific and medical research, and the arts. The Azrieli Foundation's many initiatives include: the Holocaust Survivor Memoirs Program, which collects, preserves, publishes and distributes the written memoirs of survivors in Canada; the Azrieli Institute for Educational Empowerment, an innovative program successfully working to keep at-risk youth in school; the Azrieli Fellows Program, which promotes academic excellence and leadership on the graduate level at Israeli universities; the Azrieli Music Project, which celebrates and fosters the creation of high-quality new Jewish orchestral music; and the Azrieli Neurodevelopmental Research Program, which supports advanced research on neurodevelopmental disorders, particularly Fragile X and Autism Spectrum Disorders.